TEIKYO WESTMAR UNIV. LIBR

P9-BAW-883

RECENT decades have witnessed the phenomenal growth of service industries. Currently accounting for a full 72 percent of all jobs in the United States, the service sector is the nation's most dynamic economic force.

As the mantle of leadership has passed from the manufacturing to the service-producing sector, so new trend-setting management approaches have developed among firms in the service industries. In **Managing in the Service Economy**, Harvard Business School professor James L. Heskett presents the results of an intensive analysis of many case studies to determine which management strategies have given leading service companies their clear, competitive advantages. His examples run from large multinationals such as Citibank and Carrefour to local hospitals, professional services, and transportation firms. Yet, different though their profit statements and structures may be, Heskett shows that they all share the same strategy for success, a **"strategic service vision."**

Heskett's strategic service vision is a four-point blueprint for service managers—targeting a market segment, conceptualizing how the service will be perceived by consumers, focusing on an operating strategy, and finally, designing an efficient service delivery system that transforms vision into action. Heskett supports each step with dozens of clear examples from a broad range of service industries, offering a structured set of guidelines for developing and *maintaining* competitive advantage.

In addition to his analysis of a strategic service vision, Heskett traces the development of multinational service companies, where cultural and regulatory differences may present unique challenges. He forecasts, as well, the future of the service economy—in particular, the impact of deregulation and advanced technology. These phenomena are already changing business strategies in many service industries around the world, and promise to affect others as well.

MANAGING IN THE SERVICE ECONOMY

MANAGING IN THE SERVICE ECONOMY

JAMES L. HESKETT

 HARVARD BUSINESS SCHOOL PRESS

Boston, Massachusetts • 1986

The paper used in this publication meets the requirements
of the American National Standard for Permanence of Paper
for Printed Library Materials Z39.48–1984.

Harvard Business School Press, Boston 02163

© 1986 by the President and Fellows of Harvard College
All rights reserved.

Printed in the United States of America
90 89 88

Library of Congress Cataloging-in-Publication Data

Heskett, James L.
  Managing in the service economy.

  Bibliography: p.
  Includes index.
  1. Service industries--Management. I. Title.
HD9980.5.H47 1986   658   85-30185
ISBN 0-87584-130-9

CONTENTS

Acknowledgments

My effort is based on a teaching association with the course in the management of service operations at the Harvard Business School, as well as experience as a manager, director, and consultant for firms in the service industries. As a consequence, I owe a debt of gratitude to colleagues with whom I have worked and by whom I have been influenced.

Among them are W. Earl Sasser, Jr., who developed the first course addressing the management of service operations in general (as opposed to specific industries) at the Harvard Business School; David H. Maister, Christopher H. Lovelock, and the late D. Daryl Wyckoff, with whom I have had the pleasure of teaching and working on service-related materials at the school; Theodore Levitt, who has written more sage and stimulating material about service industry management under other titles (particularly marketing) than anyone I know; and Gayton E. Germane and Nicholas A. Glaskowsky, Jr., who first introduced me to the inner workings of the transportation industries and hooked me for life.

The Division of Research at the Harvard Business School funded portions of the work on which this book is based. And the 1907 Foundation, a creation of the United Parcel Service, Inc., has for some years supported from afar a variety of research on service industries through its provision of several endowed chairs, one of which I have been fortunate to hold. But more important than this financial support, the Dean of the Harvard Business School and a highly valued associate, John H. McArthur, was willing to structure an assignment that permitted me to pull together the work of previous years.

Michele Marram and Bertil Hessel were very helpful in gathering data for this project. For their assistance in the preparation of this manuscript, I am indebted as well to Jeanette Davy and Sarah Markham.

Throughout this effort and my professional career, my wife, Marilyn, has provided a steady source of support, encouragement, and ideas. And my son, Benjamin, helped in the preparation of graphic and bibliographic information.

The unsung contributors to this work are the many inspiring, innovative, and effective managers whose efforts have resulted in the service economy we know today. They, as much as any group, have shaped our future and in so doing have provided ideas for this book.

Clearly, whatever credit this work warrants belongs to many. Complaints should be directed to me as head of the service department.

James L. Heskett
Boston, Massachusetts
March 1986

In memory of my father.

MANAGING IN THE SERVICE ECONOMY

Introduction

This book is about those things that successful managers in the service industries know and do. It is about what I call the strategic service vision—the logically organized plan for implementing new businesses and ideas—that they have. And it is about the changing environment in which they manage.

The ranks of these managers have swollen with the growth of the service sector to a size considerably larger than that of the manufacturing sector in every developed economy in the world. So in a sense, this book explores the lessons for all managers to gain from observing the most successful practitioners in the world's fastest growing economic sector.

In a landmark work,[1] Colin Clark described the transition of an economy from pre-industrial to industrial to postindustrial. He divided all economies into three sectors: primary (agricultural), secondary (manufacturing), and tertiary (services). The third sector has come to represent everything left over from the first two. Those of us who inherit Clark's legacy confront a grab bag of industries with vastly different characteristics, differing along various dimensions only in degree from manufacturing industries.

Victor Fuchs, analyzing the development of the service economy, declared "that most of the industries in it are manned by white-collar workers, that most of the industries are labor intensive, that most deal with the consumer, and that nearly all of them produce an intangible product."[2] According to Leonard Berry, "a good is an object, a device, a thing; a service is a deed, a performance, an effort . . . it is whether the essence of what is being bought is tangible or intangible that determines its classification

1

as a good or a service."[3] In fact, the word "service" is most usually associated with "intangible."

Using intangibility as the criterion, as imperfect as this may be, we can sort out which businesses count as service businesses. The list is long: finance, insurance, real estate, transportation, communications, utilities, wholesale trade, retail trade, government employment (federal, state, and local), education, health, professional services, personal services, food and lodging, and many others. Some of these services do produce tangible output, such as newspapers or food. And goods-producing businesses—mining, manufacturing, construction—require service activities such as clerical work and guard duty. But our emphasis is on what Berry terms "the essence of what is being bought."

Daniel Bell has described work in the service-oriented, postindustrial society as a "game between persons" in contrast to the "game against fabricated nature" played in the industrial society.[4] Indeed, many jobs in the service industries require more social than technical skills. And though the objective of many service strategies being created today is to limit people-to-people contact to the minimum required to "personalize" a service, the minimum will continue to be a great deal. The satisfactions for people helping people can be great and should not be underestimated as a force in providing self-fulfillment to individuals as well as in preserving a more civil (if not fully civilized) society.

Yet one goal of most service providers is to make their offerings less people-intensive—to use fewer people per unit of value added, and perhaps ultimately to reduce employment in the service sector overall. As Marvin Harris warns:

> As productivity in manufacturing and mining rose, surplus labor was drawn off into the production of information and services. What next?
>   With microchip computerization of information-and-service jobs the fastest growth industry in the United States, who can doubt that the same process is about to be repeated in the service-and-information fields? But with one difference: There is no conceivable realm of profitable employment whose expansion can make up for even modest productivity gains among the nation's sixty million service-and-information workers.[5]

To the extent that service providers succeed in accomplishing what Harris describes, the very nature of work may change as fewer jobs are created. But the most effective service providers today are those who know when personal contact is important and when it is not, those who are able to concentrate personal contact at critical moments in the service delivery process.

But why study services at all? Because growth in the service sector in the United States has been phenomenal and shows little sign of leveling off. While agricultural employment has plummeted to a low 3 percent of all employment, and goods-producing jobs total about 25 percent, service sector jobs are now a soaring 72 percent of all U.S. employment.

Between 1953 and 1984, nearly 9 out of every 10 of the 48 million nonfarm jobs added to U.S. payrolls were provided by services. By 1984, U.S. service industries were responsible for 74 percent of all nonfarm jobs, 68 percent of all nongovernment jobs, and 69 percent of all national income.[6] If we take service-related jobs in manufacturing into account, manufacturing provided only 14 percent of nonfarm employment in this country during 1984.[7] (See Appendix A, Table 1, and Figure 1 for information about long-term employment trends in service-producing, goods-producing, and farming activities.)

This spectacular service sector growth is mirrored in the performance of the stocks of major service-producing companies. I have selected a group of thirty service firm stocks, which I've called the Cambridge Service Index (see Appendix A, Table 2). They were selected on the basis of representativeness and trading activity, not on stock performance, which is consistent with the selection criteria for the Dow Jones Index of thirty industrial firms. Like the new and speculative industrials Charles Henry Dow selected in constructing his original index, several of the companies in the current Cambridge Index had little or no public trading in their stocks in 1963. One company did not even exist at that time.

While the world's investors have focused their attention on the Dow Jones Index, the Cambridge Index deserves at least as much interest as an indicator of economic activity. Comparing the Dow and the Cambridge indices, the Cambridge Services have far outperformed the Dow Jones Industrials over the past twenty years both in upturns and downturns, achieving a compounded growth rate in value more than four times that of the traditional indicator's offerings (see Appendix A, Figure 2).

The pattern is not confined to the United States. Every major developed economy, regardless of political orientation, has experi-

enced phenomenal growth in its service sector. Even Japan, believed by many to be the ultimate industrial society, has far more
service sector jobs than those in mining, construction, and manufacturing combined (see Appendix A, Table 3).

But there are reasons other than remarkable growth for us to
study service businesses. Unlike scholars of management and observers who emphasize lessons that the manufacturing sector
holds for service firms through the "industrialization" of service-
producing processes, this book makes a strong case that lessons
also go in the other direction. Managers of manufacturing firms
stand to gain new insights from their counterparts in services,
insights into such things as coordinating marketing and production, ways of substituting information for more tangible assets,
managing both demand and supply without a buffer of inventory
on which to rely, controlling quality on a multinational basis, and
organizing in new ways to understand and relate to customers and
employees in particular and people in general.

At the same time, my intention is to shed some light on a number of half-truths associated with the service industries. Among
these is the contention that services represent a drag on productivity improvements in the economy.

Some will argue that I am attempting far too much and treating
too many industries and topics. To the extent that most of the
service industries have been addressed at far greater length elsewhere, the point is valid. But overall, the service industries have
received limited systematic attention, and much of that has been
misleading. My purpose here is to identify common threads that
characterize many of the industries in the polyglot of service activities, distinguish them from industrial activities, and provide insights into effective management that managers in both sectors
can use.

The first two chapters of this book are about the elements of a
strategic service vision. Chapters 3 through 7 discuss the key issues in integrating the elements successfully, issues that suggest
interesting lessons for manufacturing firms as well. The multinational development of service businesses is the concern of Chapter
8. Chapter 9 ranges over future prospects for service industries. I
offer some concluding remarks in the final chapter.

CHAPTER ONE

A Strategic Service Vision
Basic Elements

In 1960, Marcel Fournier, operator of a single small retail store in Annecy, France, took careful note of a basic structural change in French society: the traditional consumer was being replaced.[1]

In the traditional French family, there was one wage earner, typically male, and his wife who shopped for groceries daily, and often twice daily, very near her home. This was not just custom, for the family had no car, or if it did, the woman of the house could not drive it. Further, the family either owned no refrigerator or had a very small one. The European emphasis on quality and freshness in food did not permit much buying ahead; it required frequent shopping at small, neighborhood stores supplied daily by wholesalers making small, inefficient deliveries at high prices passed on to consumers.

But the traditional French family was gradually being replaced by the more modern one, often headed by younger adults born after World War II. Its two wage earners owned a car and a large refrigerator; they had no time to shop for groceries before every meal or even daily, and in any case neighborhood stores' hours did not coincide with business hours. Social needs were fulfilled in part by activities other than shopping, and younger couples were dissatisfied with the slow, expensive service provided by their neighborhood merchants who had to be visited one-by-one in provisioning the household.

Taking cues from the American development of the supermarket and the successful opening of his own supermarket in 1960 in Annecy, Marcel Fournier decided that the France of the 1960s offered an even greater opportunity than had the United States of the 1930s and 1940s, one that called for a bold, preemptive strike against potential competition. As a result, he opened the first *hypermarché* near Paris and began developing second, tenth, and thirtieth stores in rapid succession. These stores did not merely match the American supermarket model—they were five to eight times larger. Located as much as twenty-five miles from large cities and named *Carrefour*, French for crossroad, these stores featured packaged grocery products sold in larger packs at prices a fraction of those at neighborhood mom-and-pop stores. Produce was offered in profusion, often in palletized containers brought directly to the floor of a specially constructed Carrefour store by lift trucks, creating an impression of freshness unequaled elsewhere. And smaller spaces in these huge, attractively decorated and lit buildings covering as much as six acres were leased to other retailers of services and nonfood items to provide one-stop shopping for the modern French family longing for it and willing to drive relatively long distances to get it.

The Carrefour vision was not just one of a modern, efficient, distribution system for a changing French society. It was planned so that grocery-product suppliers would not only provide trade credit for packaged groceries but would also help supply money for the construction of the stores, the working capital needed for their operation, and even the dividends paid to owners of the company. All this was made possible by Carrefour's seemingly logical request to its suppliers that it be given exactly the same trade credit terms as its smaller competitors, no better or no worse. Since these terms were extremely liberal to allow for slow inventory turnover in the mom-and-pop stores, they were much more liberal than those required by a modern supermarket and incredibly greater than those required by a *hypermarché*.

So, with ninety days to pay for goods that it could sell to consumers in twenty, Carrefour had seventy days of money with which to operate its stores and even construct new ones. The faster the rate of construction, the greater the opportunity to earn trade credit. Carrefour's meteoric growth was not constrained by financing. The validity of this growth strategy was confirmed by another phenomenon that Carrefour's management did not fully anticipate.

As might be expected, a nation of shopkeepers would not accept the development of the *hypermarché* without protest. Carrefour became a target. Efforts to stop its development appeared through zoning and other types of legislation. One Carrefour store caught fire and burned under mysterious circumstances. But had Carrefour's management planned them, the results could hardly have been more beneficial. As the first in each major market with an immense store, Carrefour was held exempt from the resulting restrictive legislation and became, in effect, shielded from its competitors.

Thus, by targeting a segment of the market, developing a concept to serve some of the needs of the segment for convenient one-stop shopping, developing an operating strategy that allowed it to finance its rapid growth with its suppliers' money, and by designing and building a service delivery system centered on huge stores and advanced materials-handling methods, Carrefour fashioned a service enterprise that has grown and flourished to this day.

Carrefour is thus an excellent example of how service firms become large and successful through the strategic vision of their founders and managers. It also provides an example of the elements of a strategic service vision that characterize all leading service firms: a targeted market, a well-defined service concept, a focused operating strategy, and a well-designed service delivery system.

The basic elements of a strategic service vision are listed in Figure 1-1. Relevant questions are listed below each element. Thinking about possible answers to these questions can help form the outline of a conceptual framework for a strategic service vision.

THE TARGETED MARKET SEGMENT

A service cannot be all things to all people. Unlike product manufacturers, service organizations can have considerable difficulty delivering more than one "product," more than one type or level of service, at one time. Groups or "segments" of customers

Target Market Segments	Service Concept	Operating Strategy	Service Delivery System
What are common characteristics of important market segments?	What are important elements of the service to be provided, stated in terms of results produced for customers?	What are important elements of the strategy? Operations? Financing? Marketing? Organization? Human resources? Control?	What are important features of the service delivery system, including: The role of people? Technology? Equipment? Facilities? Layout? Procedures?
What dimensions can be used to segment the market? Demographic? Psychographic?	How are these elements supposed to be perceived by the target market segment? By the market in general? By employees? By others?	On which will the most effort be concentrated? Where will investments be made?	What capacity does it provide? Normally? At peak levels?
How important are various segments?	How is the service concept perceived?	How will quality and cost be controlled? Measures? Incentives? Rewards?	To what extent does it: Help insure quality standards? Differentiate the service from competition? Provide barriers to entry by competitors?
What needs does each have? How well are these needs being served? In what manner? By whom?	What efforts does this suggest in terms of the manner in which the service is: Designed? Delivered? Marketed?	What results will be expected vs. competition in terms of: Quality of service? Cost profile? Productivity? Morale/loyalty of servers?	

Figure 1-1

Basic Elements of a Strategic Service Vision

must be singled out for a particular service, their needs determined, and a service concept developed that provides a competitive advantage for the server in the eyes of those to be served.

SEGMENTATION

Segmentation is the process of identifying groups of customers with enough characteristics in common to make possible the design and presentation of a product or service each group needs. Just as Carrefour's founders identified a large group of young adults in France with life-styles and needs distinctly different from those of their elders, other firms have done the same.

SAS, Swissair, and Lufthansa in Europe carry relatively higher proportions of high-margin business travelers than their competitors because they have identified business travelers' special needs and have designed services to meet them better. These companies stress schedules to meet business needs, on-time performance, a business-class service intermediate to economy and first-class services with features conducive to work on board, and back-up ground services in the event of late arrival or other unexpected events. Other airlines have been forced to follow suit.

Demographic Dimensions. Age, income, education level, family size, and location are a few of the many demographic dimensions on which a market may be segmented. Each may have different relevance to a particular business. McDonald's tracks families with children below the age of fifteen more carefully than young couples, although recently it has sought locations and food service concepts that may appeal to young couples as well. H & R Block has designed its tax preparation service to meet the needs of those with less complex tax returns and limited confidence in their ability to prepare their own returns.

Demographic information is usually readily available and easily obtained; unfortunately, it is often less relevant than more difficult-to-obtain and costly psychographic information.

Psychographic Dimensions. Psychographics describe the way people think and the actions prompted by those thoughts. These dimensions define levels of pleasure, fear, innovativeness, boredom, and vanity, to name a few, in various segments of the population. They help explain the way people act and the way they live, often cutting across demographic dimensions to identify groups of customers with common behavior patterns in their purchases of goods or services.

One important psychographic dimension whose understanding has provided the foundation for more than one highly successful service is that of perceived risk, including perceived economic, social, legal, or medical risks. Research has suggested repeatedly that customers associate risk more highly with the purchase of services than with goods;[2] customers for services often feel they have less information about services than about goods.[3] Other sources of perceived risk have been the nonstandard nature of many services, the lack of evaluative criteria, and the absence of or difficulties with guarantees against poor performance.

Persons displaying high levels of perceived risks often lack knowledge or self-confidence about a particular product or service or suffer from a high level of exposure. They often are quite willing to pay higher-than-usual prices for properly designed services that yield higher-than-usual margins and profits. Physicians have understood this implicitly for years. The low state of medical knowledge and the high levels of perceived risks in nearly all patients account in part for the high and rapidly escalating prices for medical services. Only recently have people begun to "comparison shop" for health care.

Polls repeatedly rate auto repairmen low for trustworthiness. And recently, within the rapidly growing segment described as single, young, working adults under age thirty, a large segment of auto owners has been created having high levels of education, little knowledge of mechanics, and a basic dislike for being placed in the hands of an unknown repairman who would be difficult to trust. This large, growing segment of the population is interested in and willing to pay for an auto repair process they can understand and trust.

The Lex Service Group, a distributor as well as a retailer of fine motor cars in England, has for some years practiced risk reduction with owners of expensive autos by providing capable mechanics whom customers can trust to service their cars. Lex mechanics go out of their way to explain work to be done, both at the present and in the future; they maintain well-organized and clean facilities; and they identify themselves with their work and stand behind it. These service policies are regarded as equally important as auto design and styling in the segments of the market targeted by Lex. The result is that Lex's prices, margins, and profits on service are relatively high, along with their customers' satisfaction.

SELECTING THE TARGET

The selection of a particular market segment as a target for the design, delivery, and marketing of a service may depend, among other factors, on the size of the segment, its needs, the extent to which these needs are being met (or more important, not being met), and the capabilities of the proposed service for meeting such needs.

What makes a market segment attractive? If a firm wants to deliver a basic service at low cost, it will look for customers valuing low prices. But purveyors of a highly differentiated, high-cost service will focus on two other dimensions of overriding importance: the rate of growth in available margins (whether through increasing total sales or increasing the margin on each sale), and the relative sensitivity of that segment's members to the "design" as opposed to the price of a service.

The rate of growth in available margins suggests the profit potential in the segment. Segments whose members value some element of design over price are less sensitive to price. They offer an attractive, high-margin target to the firm able to deliver a service designed to meet these customers' needs better than its competition.

Consider the traditional ways banks segment the airline market. Money is regarded as a commodity by those who borrow or lend it. Price (the interest rate) is therefore thought to be what drives many commercial borrowers to select a lender. Differences of one-fourth or even one-eighth of a percentage point in the interest rate can sometimes move a borrower from one bank to another. In lending money to airlines the problem is compounded by the fact that there are so many willing lenders for the small number of successful airlines and so few willing lenders for the larger number of airlines with uncertain futures. Thus, when asked about dimensions on which to segment the airline market, some bank lending officers will respond that there is only one: whether an airline is a good risk or a bad one. Unfortunately, because of competition among lenders, it is difficult to realize a good return on a loan to a "good" risk in the airline industry. Poor risks are willing to pay higher interest rates or to entertain creative ideas just to get the loan.

The traditional ways of segmenting the airline market did not serve the lending group of a major bank that we'll call First Metropolitan. Not until its members looked into elements distinguishing one supposedly poor loan risk in the airline industry from another did opportunities for a differentiated lending strategy appear. Some of the poor risks resulted from a recent start-up in the newly deregulated airline industry; others resulted from what were perceived as poor route structures. Some were the product of what was perceived as bad management. Still others were apparent from weak financial statements, often involving undercapitalization.

Within this group a subgroup with clearly superior strategies, often based on attractive routes and clearly defined management objectives, was identified. Over time, these airlines were judged good future risks for lenders, and few of them were sensitive to the long-term costs of the money they needed for success in the short-term future. In advance of its competition, therefore, the lending group at First Metropolitan began structuring loans of relatively low immediate cost to meet the needs of these more attractive airlines that competing lenders generally assessed as poor risks.

Only by examining dimensions for segmentation in greater depth did the bank's airline lending group discover a business opportunity. Without its knowledge of the industry, the group's success would not have been possible.

Figure 1-2 displays the critical dimensions identified by the airline lending group at First Metropolitan. Similarly organized information can prove helpful in guiding thinking about the selection of market segments on which a firm might focus its effort.

Because Figure 1-2 summarizes a great deal of information, two cautions are necessary. First, such a matrix can be prepared only after dimensions for segmenting the market are identified. It requires an examination of the reasons why a segment might have strong long-run margin potential. Second, it requires an interpretation of what "design" means among members of a particular market segment.

Two competitors may view potential markets somewhat differently, depending on their views of themselves and potential cus-

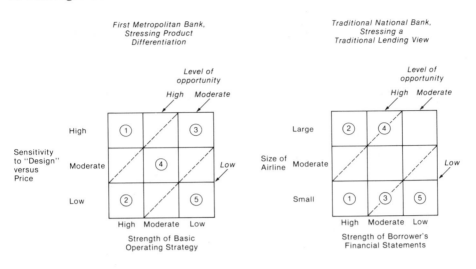

First Metropolitan Bank,
Stressing Product
Differentiation

Traditional National Bank,
Stressing a
Traditional Lending View

① = Segment 1. composed of small airlines with well-focused fleets and route structures. strong management. and limited financing.
② = Segment 2. composed of large. well-managed airlines with ready availability of alternative sources of funds.
③ = Segment 3. composed of small airlines with poorly focused fleets and route structures but capable management and limited financing.
④ = Segment 4. composed of large airlines with moderately well-focused fleets and route structures. acceptable management. and moderate access to funds.
⑤ = Segment 5. composed of small airlines with poorly focused fleets and route structures. weak management. and limited financing.

Figure 1-2
The Relative Attractiveness of Borrowers to Two Banks Lending to Airlines

tomers, as the comparison between First Metro and Traditional National Bank in Figure 1-2 suggests. One might have the ability (and willingness) to differentiate its loan package, and the other might tend to loan with a traditional bias toward size and financial capacity.

By identifying those "poor risk" airlines with relatively strong long-run potential and by assessing the needs of each as well as its willingness to meet those needs, the lenders at First Metro realized higher interest rates with only a small increment of risk in relation to their competitors at the Traditional National Bank. Given the ability to structure deals involving convertible debentures, for example, the group possessed a certain strength in relation to several of its competitors. But the strongest element of differentiation was First Metro's willingness to lend money in the light of perceptions yielded by its analysis. This required a well-supported presentation to senior bank lending officers accustomed only to an orthodox approach to the market. By then it had become clear to the lending officers at the First Metro Bank that they were not dealing with a commodity to be dispensed at the lowest interest rate.

MOVING TARGETS

The same person may be associated with different market segments while engaged in various activities or from one moment to the next. The business executive who flies business class during working hours often selects economy class service when traveling on a family vacation; and a family's financial needs are believed to change from one stage of its life cycle to another in the manner shown in Figure 1-3.

This "segment mobility" can create problems for the firm seeking to serve more than one segment with the same personnel or equipment. The best service firms recognize this and take it into account in designing and marketing their services, or they monitor potential problems of segment mobility before these become too serious. American Airlines watched its quarterly measure of service perceived by its highly valued business travelers plummet during the summer months several years ago, when it introduced a three-class service that included a very low-priced, minimal economy class. Its business travelers, experiencing the economy class while on vacation with their families, had perhaps unconsciously viewed this as a deterioration of American's usually good service. The three-class service was eliminated in a matter of days.

DISCRETE AND NONDISCRETE SEGMENT BEHAVIOR

American Airline's problem characterizes that of many service providers unable to partition their services and customers into discrete groups. When services are consumed at the point of delivery and in the company of other customers, service companies may find it difficult to offer the same "product" to distinctly different segments, as manufacturers of products from Cadillacs to dog food have been able to do. As Christopher Lovelock has said, "In the case of high-contact, shared services . . . the nature of the client base is readily apparent. . . . Two or more distinct market segments

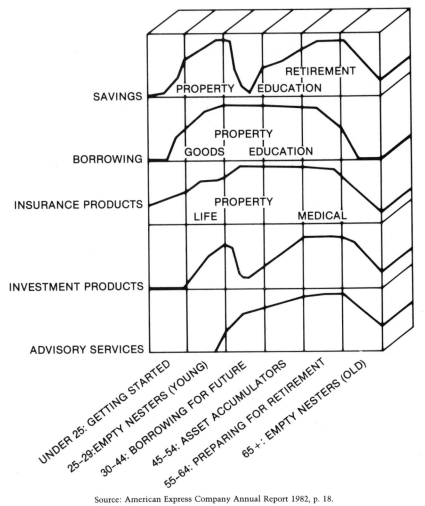

SAVINGS

RETIREMENT

PROPERTY EDUCATION

BORROWING

PROPERTY
GOODS EDUCATION

INSURANCE PRODUCTS

PROPERTY
LIFE MEDICAL

INVESTMENT PRODUCTS

ADVISORY SERVICES

UNDER 25: GETTING STARTED

25-29:EMPTY NESTERS (YOUNG)

30-44: BORROWING FOR FUTURE

45-54: ASSET ACCUMULATORS

55-64: PREPARING FOR RETIREMENT

65+: EMPTY NESTERS (OLD)

Source: American Express Company Annual Report 1982, p. 18.

Figure 1-3
Consumer Financial Services Life Cycle

may each contribute importantly to the organization's success, yet they may not mix well."[4]

A hotel offering quiet, genteel surroundings to the upscale business traveler can hardly afford to accommodate noisy, demanding tour groups during the week. But by Friday night, most business travelers have returned home, giving the hotel the opportunity to build patronage through weekend "family packages." Likewise, a radio station may offer programming appealing to commuters during the morning and afternoon "drive times" while changing its format to appeal to other segments the rest of the day. The risk, of course, is that members of the company's target segment may arrive or tune in at the wrong time, gaining a somewhat different impression of their favored service. It is a risk that has to be assessed carefully and assumed occasionally if high facility utilization is to be attained.

THE WELL-DEFINED SERVICE CONCEPT

A service concept describes the way an organization would like to have its service perceived by its customers and employees, and by its shareholders and lenders as well. This is management's way of answering the familiar question, "What business are we in?" or at least, "What business do we want the customer to think we are in?" In leading service firms, the response is phrased and communicated to customers, employees, and others very carefully.

The demand among wealthy tourists for luxurious long-distance travel by train in Europe declined significantly with the development of dependable air passenger service. Large, increasingly nationalized rail systems no longer met the needs of such potential travelers because they concentrated on providing dependable service over shorter distances to large numbers of passengers interested in economy. As a result, famous luxury trains gradually disappeared.

While the demand for luxurious surface travel declined, it did not disappear. A number of people longed to travel at least once in the old grand tradition, whether for variety, to satisfy vanity, or from an intense interest in railroad history. James B. Sherwood, acting on behalf of the Sea Containers Group in England, perceived this desire to be large enough to support the revival of at least one such train, the Venice Simplon-Orient-Express. In 1981 Sea Containers reintroduced a successful luxury service between London and Venice, utilizing carefully restored railroad carriages, offering all-sleeping-car service, featuring the finest cuisine, and encouraging "guests" to dress formally for dinner. Its target market segment is large enough to support it. The Venice Simplon-Orient-Express, Ltd., concentrating on the segment desiring only the greatest luxury, has been able to design a service uniquely capable of meeting its needs.[5] What's the service concept here? Certainly not transportation but rather a unique travel experience with heavy doses of nostalgia. But it's a concept that requires careful design and communication to potential customers.

RESULTS PRODUCED FOR CUSTOMERS

Dun & Bradstreet does not provide its clients with financial services. It offers lenders and investors an objective and accurate source of credit information, security, and even "peace of mind." It offers companies for which it provides financial reports access to trade credit or to sources of financial support.

If communicated in these terms to customers, a service concept can help potential customers evaluate and select alternative services. And when communicated clearly to employees, a service concept can focus attention on the importance of certain aspects of the server's work. At Dun & Bradstreet, employees universally recognize the importance of accuracy in financial and other information they compile and disseminate. By communicating its expectations, the company encourages careful work.

CUSTOMERS' PERCEPTIONS

If a firm sends potential customers messages that are consistent with its service concept, customers should form desired perceptions of the product. But where the messages are complex and of many types, they can be confusing.

In service industries, a customer reads, hears, or views advertising prior to buying the product and may even visit the factory and interact with one or more members of the server's work force in the process of purchasing a service. And because they involve people and their behavior, services often provide more vivid topics of conversation among persons seeking or giving purchasing advice than do products.

Wendy's International popularized the concept of the "up-scale hamburger" cooked to order "hot 'n juicy" from high-quality ingredients and served in inviting surroundings in the "old-fashioned" way at prices higher than its competitors. To communicate the concept, the company not only advertised most of these features but also designed its facilities to include a highly visible grill, carpeting, tables and chairs, Tiffany lamps, and large windows. In this context, the name Wendy, appropriate for the founder's daughter but considered unusual for a fast-food chain, fitted the customer's perception of an old-fashioned product and service.[6]

An exclusive financial advisory service cannot be delivered by poorly dressed advisors from run-down offices far from the financial district, no matter how good the advice actually dispensed. On the other hand, an advisory service intended for people with less than the highest incomes may discourage potential clients with premises that look too expensive. Accordingly, Sears has located the offices of its financial advisory service in its retail stores, making them as accessible and inviting as possible to customers who may be using such services for the first time. Banks, too, have adopted a more friendly image aimed at the middle-income customer by placing their loan desks near tellers' windows and in locations visible from the street.

All of these efforts by the best-managed service firms convey the same message and reinforce the desired customer perception. If not, the service sites are redesigned.

THE FOCUSED OPERATING STRATEGY

An operating strategy that sets forth the way the service concept will be achieved is the product of many decisions about operations, financing, marketing, human resources, and control. Just as a firm rarely *can* do all things well, so rarely *must* it do all things well. The most successful firms have identified those elements of strategic importance and have concentrated their efforts, investments, and controls on them. These firms effectively deliver results promised in the service concept while achieving internal goals associated with people, costs, and profits. Sometimes, the development of an effective operating strategy provides the key that unlocks the barrier to successful performance in an entire industry.

In recent years many large banks have sought to improve their share of banking business in the so-called "middle market," comprising firms with annual sales in the range of $5 million to $100 million—highly attractive and rapidly-growing accounts. Middle-market borrowers, however, often need loans sooner and with more flexible terms than their larger counterparts; often they cannot supply audited statements required by the loan officers and committees of many large "money center" banks operating commercial loan offices in major cities.

Mark Twain Bancshares, a St. Louis-based banking organization, has targeted this middle market in its primary markets of St. Louis and Kansas City and developed an operating strategy consistent with the target.[7] Instead of organizing itself in the traditional manner, with branch managers relying heavily on headquarters for many operating decisions on interest rate policies, loan approvals, and other matters, Mark Twain operates a number of banks with some degree of autonomy, each headed by a president and board of directors. The president is given profit responsibility and, within limits, authority to make independent decisions for his or her bank. Board members are chosen from among the chief executive officers of middle-market companies, the bank's marketing targets. At last count, the number of such board members throughout the Mark Twain organization was approaching 300.

Through a strategy yielding good knowledge of a targeted market, Mark Twain is able to react faster and more flexibly to its middle-market customers' borrowing needs than its competitors. If necessary, it can do so without requiring its customers to supply audited financial statements. And it is able to do so without incurring the risk that its larger competitors' restrictive policies and procedures are designed to minimize, because it knows its targeted customers, many of whom are also directors. Mark Twain thus holds a dominant share of the middle market in cities in which it operates against much larger banks with less well-focused operating strategies.

Focused operating strategies are found at the heart of successful operations in all service industries. Many airlines, for example, have adopted so-called "hub-and-spoke" strategies: flights from "spoke" cities are scheduled to arrive at and depart from a "hub" terminal on a schedule that allows passengers to catch connecting flights without changing terminals or even airlines. To the extent that an airline can establish and provide the dominant service at a hub, it can both control its hub service effectively and provide the most frequent and convenient connecting schedules for its incoming passengers, who often continue by air beyond the hub. Perhaps most important, the airline can obtain a larger share of a passenger's business by discouraging transfers to other airlines. Although the passenger traveling through a hub might prefer direct flights from origin to destination, the greater frequency of service and economy offered by a hub-and-spoke strategy, especially to those people flying routes on small "spokes," makes the overall service package more attractive to customers.

THE WELL-DESIGNED SERVICE DELIVERY SYSTEM

An ingenious operating strategy intended to provide a service aimed at a particular market segment is useless if the delivery system does not work. Systems that deliver successfully consist of well-thought-out jobs for people with the capabilities and attitudes necessary for their successful performance; equipment, facilities, and layouts for effective customer and work flow; and carefully developed procedures aimed at a common set of clearly defined objectives. They provide sufficient capacity (neither too little nor too much) to meet most commonly experienced levels of demand efficiently. They can help reduce customers' perceptions of risk. And the delivery systems themselves often help insure that standards for service quality are met, that services perceived by customers are differentiated from the competition, and that barriers to competitive entry are built.

A good example is the Xerox Corporation's system for providing service and maintenance support to its copying machine sales and leasing business. To service some two million machines owned or leased by its customers worldwide,[8] Xerox employs some 26,000 service representatives whose tasks, supporting equipment and facilities, and performance measures and rewards have been carefully thought out.

The original design of the system benefited from the fact that all Xerox machines were leased under an agreement that provided a royalty to Xerox for each page produced by a customer with a machine. Hence, machine failure resulted both in inconvenience for the customer and in potential lost revenue for Xerox. It also carried with it the risk that the customer would cancel the lease for the machine. The cost to Xerox of poor service, by customer type and location, could be estimated and compared with the incremental cost to the company of varying levels of service.

The economics of losing business through machine downtime led Xerox's management to establish delivery-system goals and capacity plans to insure that, on average, machine downtime due to lack of availability of parts would not exceed thirty minutes. In order to achieve this, Xerox had to design and implement a highly responsive parts-supply system with affordable costs.

Of the many alternatives available to Xerox for providing timely repair service, two help illustrate the point. First, trucks could be outfitted with nearly all the components and tools needed to repair even the largest of Xerox's machines. Service representatives, responding to requests for service under this strategy, would be largely self-sufficient. Or, service representatives might instead drive automobiles with a smaller stock of the most common and compact Xerox parts and tools in their trunk compartments, a stock optimized by a computer analysis of Xerox's repair experiences. Determining by telephone or observation that the job required a part not in the automobile, the service rep could phone a local Xerox stocking point and either pick up the part or have it delivered by cab.

The company chose the second of these alternatives. Given the number of service reps required, it was not feasible to support each one with a truck and a nearly complete inventory. Automobiles, on the other hand, had trunks large enough to accommodate the computer-optimized field inventory but small enough to discourage the human tendency of service reps to carry extra "buffer" stocks.

Because of Xerox's service concept and customers' perceptions, it was decided that service reps should wear suits. This decision further favored automobiles; trucks were most typically driven by individuals in long white smocks or worse. Finally, briefcases rather than tool kits were supplied.

The most personal and possibly most effective service could have been provided by assigning individual accounts to be serviced by each representative, but with the stringent goals for timely service, this would require too much reserve capacity. Lead representatives were therefore designated for each account, particularly for routine maintenance. They were sometimes supplanted at times of emergencies when customers were thought to prefer timely service to a familiar face.

Procedures had long since been developed to make a service call most productive in time and results. When it became clear that certain procedures could save entire service calls and could be carried out by someone with no technical background and limited training, Xerox established the Key Operator Program. Customers were encouraged to nominate employees for training by Xerox service reps to become Key Operators, responsible for performing simple problem diagnosis and repair before calling a service rep for more expert assistance. More recently, the company has begun offering an Advanced Customer Training course in which employees of customers owning the largest machines learn a more comprehensive set of maintenance and problem-solving tasks involving simple tools and procedures. Thus, customer involvement in the process has worked to the benefit of both Xerox and its customers.

Given its emphasis on fixing the machine properly on the first visit, Xerox had to design methods of performance measurement and compensation carefully. Quality rather than the number of service calls was stressed, and all but a small proportion of a service rep's income was based on salary. Quality control has been based on a number of measurements. Foremost among these has been the Customer Satisfaction Survey, mailed regularly to sample populations of Xerox customers. Close attention has also been paid to the number of copies made between service calls as a measurement of reliability and, by implication, call quality.

From the beginning, Xerox was forced to think long and hard about the role of people, equipment, facilities, and procedures in its service delivery system. It had to determine ways to provide capacity sufficient to meet its stringent service goals, and it had to devise methods of measuring and rewarding good performance, both for its own employees and for certain employees of its customers.

Xerox probably overdesigned its service delivery system at the outset. After all, its major competitive advantage lay in a marvelous set of patents on xerography that gave it a long head start. But today nearly all of Xerox's pathbreaking patents have expired, and some competitors are producing equipment with similar capabilities. Yet none can afford to match Xerox on service covering wide geographic areas (versus small pockets of business concentration). Xerox's service army (literally larger than an army division) is well entrenched, backed up by equipment, procedures, and controls, and it provides the company with its most important barrier to competition.

Service delivery system design can play a major role in reducing real risk as well as customers' perceptions of high risks associated with many services. Consider the findings reported several years ago by Dr. Kenneth N. Barker, then head of the Department of Pharmacy Care Systems at Auburn University. He estimated that patients did not receive their prescribed medication or dosage in 10 percent of the cases he studied. To combat the problem many hospitals have adopted "unit-dose" dispensing programs in which specific doses, labeled and ready to administer, are sent from a hospital's pharmacy to the nursing stations. According to Barker, "Patients in other hospitals can expect on the average one error a day in their medication."[9]

In response to generally high levels of customer distrust associated with auto repair, some repair shops have initiated such features as posted prices for standard tasks, service representatives who take time to explain the nature of the work to be done and efforts necessary to complete it satisfactorily, and dependable estimates of completion time. At Midas Muffler it is standard procedure for the mechanic to take the customer through a brief process in which the vehicle is inspected, the problem identified, the solution proposed, and the cost estimated. This provides both information and reassurance.

Customers' anxieties result from uncertainty about what to expect, the inability to obtain visual and other cues that might provide a guide through the service "maze," and the general feeling that they have almost no control over the service process. One study found, for example, that 20 percent of the customers arriving at the new Dallas–Fort Worth International Airport (reputedly the latest in airport design) could not find their way to the baggage claim area. Additional people had to be hired to direct them.[10] One airline operating out of the same terminal found that the building engendered high anxiety because it obscured the airplanes from view until passengers had completed all but the final boarding steps. Spaces that are hard to see into, like many bank buildings, have been associated with customer anxiety. One senior manager has asked in print why such important elements of a service are left in the hands of interior designers.[11]

Uniforms exemplify the need for attention to detail in designing a service delivery system. A uniform provides visible evidence when little else is available about the possible quality of a service.

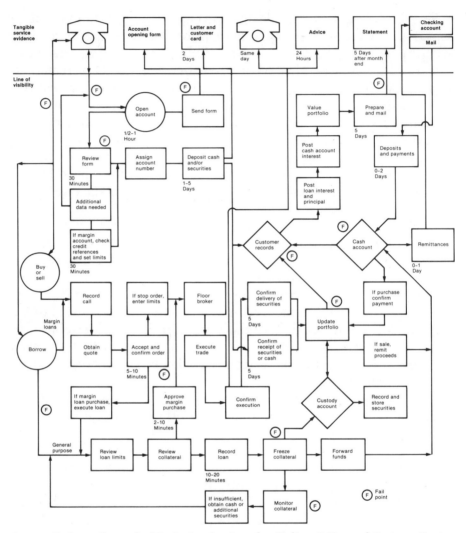

Source: G. Lynn Shostack, "Designing Services that Deliver." *Harvard Business Review,* January-February 1984, 133–139, at 138. Reprinted with permission.

Figure 1-4
Blueprint for a Service Delivery System of a Discount Brokerage Operation

This has been shown to be of particular importance for customers of professional services, but it is significant in at least the first purchase of many other services.[12] When uniforms also display some form of identification, either the wearer's name or a number, the customer is given a small but important sense of having some control over the transaction. (With this in mind, the French government recently instituted a program to require many of its civil servants to wear name tags, thus providing relief to those forced to deal with anonymous government employees who traditionally serve the state rather than its citizens.) Finally, the uniform serves as a form of control: it reminds the server, who is often carrying out customer-contact work without direct supervision, of the quality of performance expected.[13] It is one detail that leading service firm managers understand well.

Some of the more effective service delivery systems have in fact been designed by those who must manage and work in them. Lynn Shostack, senior vice president at Bankers Trust Company, has given a great deal of thought to the process of designing the delivery system.[14] An approach that she calls "blueprinting" involves the diagramming of all components of a service transaction, as shown for a discount brokerage service in Figure 1-4. "Fail points," those steps most likely to cause problems, are identified so that they can be given special attention and support through extra staffing, facility layout, or other means. Execution standards for each step are set and calibrated. Finally, efforts are made to see and measure the service as the customer sees it (above the line of visibility shown in Figure 1-4). Shostack emphasizes, however, that the customer's view should be regarded as only one element in an effort to design and control the service experience; it should be effective as well from the points of view of the server and the server's employer.

CHAPTER TWO

A Strategic Service Vision
Integrative Elements

Perhaps the most successful hospital in the world is located just outside Toronto, Ontario. It opens its doors to all patients suffering from a common affliction, and it attracts patients from the local area, the United States, Europe, and other parts of the world. It specializes in surgery and its staff performs more than 7,000 operations per year. The staff is well trained and the hospital's facilities are clean and well maintained.[1]

Shouldice Hospital, privately operated, is among the most profitable anywhere, yet the hospital makes its services available at a fraction of the total cost of alternative care facilities available to its patients. Patients are so satisfied and loyal that as many as 1,500 travel varying distances each year to attend a reunion sponsored by the hospital. Measured by the success rate of their operations, physicians at Shouldice are at least twelve times more effective than their counterparts elsewhere. The hospital's management demonstrates the basic elements of a strategic service vision.

The Shouldice Hospital targets its market segments not in terms of age, area of residence, or state of mind but in terms of those afflicted with one type of medical problem: the inguinal hernia. A small target? Operations to correct inguinal hernias are the second most frequently performed in the world, representing perhaps a

27

million surgical operations per year. The way in which Shouldice targets its market allows it to hire and train specialists and build highly focused facilities, thus enabling it to offer the highest quality of service available anywhere at prices that represent excellent value.

By concentrating on one type of operation, Shouldice is able to employ an operating strategy called the Shouldice Method: It uses local anesthetics and a specially developed procedure of suturing to insure rapid and effective patient recovery. The procedure could be patented if the hospital's doctors were inclined to limit its use. They are not so inclined, even though each of them performs more operations of this type than doctors anywhere else. Shouldice has also developed a postoperative regimen of exercise that, along with the avoidance of general anesthetics, allows most of its patients to return to work in half the time required by alternative procedures.

A market target of patients who basically are not sick allows Shouldice to incorporate certain features into its facility that encourage exercise and rapid recovery. Hospital rooms are devoid of such luxuries as showers, telephones, and television sets. Patients must walk to reach these facilities, often climbing stairs whose risers have been reduced in height to make stepping up a little less painful. Shouldice's facilities also offer twenty-seven acres of carefully tended grounds for strolling, and the hospital itself is carpeted to facilitate walking and cleaned with disinfectants that do not smell of "hospital."

The success of Shouldice rests on its having been developed around a strategic service vision involving *integrative elements* as well. Integrative elements provide guidelines for action in a fully developed framework for planning and implementation in a service business: positioning, leveraging of value over cost, and integration of strategy and systems.

Shouldice Hospital is carefully positioned against its competition. It screens its clients carefully, using both a questionnaire mailed to patients prior to admittance and an entry examination. It accepts only patients in relatively good health who have hernias that can be repaired without a general anesthetic. This accounts for some of the superiority of Shouldice's results in relation to its competitors.

But Shouldice has done a number of other things to achieve maximum leverage of perceived value over the cost of its service. It has standardized its operating procedures, and it manages demand through an appointment process geared to available capacity. The hospital manages capacity by releasing rapidly recovering patients early. It controls quality by grouping operating rooms to encourage consultation and exchange of information among its doctors and by referring patients with recurring difficulties back to the doctor who performed the operation. Doctors are paid a good wage but less than most would be able to make as medical entrepreneurs. Staff costs are lowered by involving patients in their own therapy as well as in that of others. Patients begin their own therapy by accepting the surgeons' almost-legendary invitations to walk from the operating table; they begin counseling incoming patients within hours after the completion of their own operations at a bedtime function called "tea and cookies" (an unforgettable experience for Shouldice alumni).

Finally, the operating strategy and service delivery system are integrated at Shouldice. This is reflected in the design of the buildings, in policies, in procedures, and in job design. Because the patients are usually otherwise healthy, doctors work regular days that end at 4 P.M. Only occasionally are they on call, a routine appealing to those, in the words of one administrator, "who like to see their children grow up." Doctors aspiring to make individual reputations are not hired. Communal dining, in which everyone has to pick up his or her own meal in the kitchen, fosters a family-type atmosphere. Nursing and even housekeeping jobs involve not only the usual "bed pan duty" but patient counseling as well. And the hospital laundry is staffed by only two people because patients are encouraged to spend so little time in bed. As might be expected, employee turnover is extremely low and morale high.

These integrative elements—positioning, leveraging of value over cost, and integration of strategy and systems—provide as much insight into the success of Shouldice Hospital as do the basic elements of its strategy.

The integrative elements of a strategic service vision are shown as part of its overall scheme, including both basic and integrative elements in Figure 2-1. Relevant questions are listed below each element. Thinking about possible answers to these questions can provide a framework for the analysis of a service operation as well as an explanation of its success (or lack of it) in a wide range of service firms.[2]

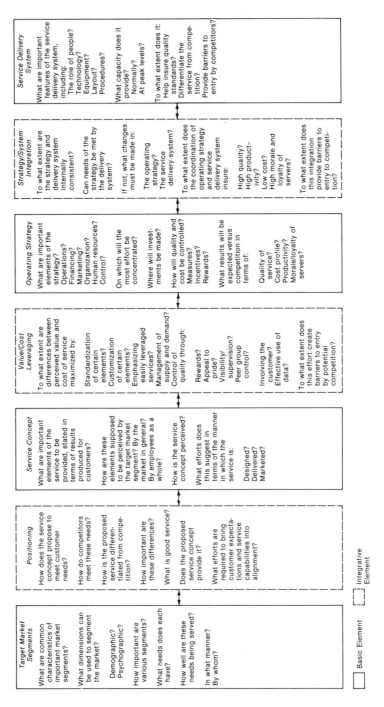

Figure 2-1

Basic and Integrative Elements of a Strategic Service Vision

Target Market Segments

What are common characteristics of important market segments?

What dimensions can be used to segment the market?

Demographic? Psychographic?

How important are various segments?

What needs does each have?

How well are these needs being served?

In what manner? By whom?

Positioning

How does the service concept propose to meet customer needs?

How do competitors meet these needs?

How is the proposed service differentiated from competition?

How important are these differences?

What is good service?

Does the proposed service concept provide it?

What efforts are required to bring customer expectations and service capabilities into alignment?

Service Concept

What are important elements of the service to be provided, stated in terms of results produced for customers?

How are these elements supposed to be perceived by the target market segment? By the market in general? By employees as a whole?

How is the service concept perceived?

What efforts does this suggest in terms of the manner in which the service is:

Designed? Delivered? Marketed?

Value/Cost Leveraging

To what extent are differences between perceived value and cost of service maximized by:

Standardization of certain elements?

Customization of certain elements?

Emphasizing easily leveraged services?

Management of supply and demand?

Control of quality through:

Rewards? Appeal to pride? Visibility/ supervision? Peer group control?

Involving the customer? Effective use of data?

To what extent does this effort create barriers to entry by potential competition?

Operating Strategy

What are important elements of the strategy? Operations? Financing? Marketing? Organization? Human resources? Control?

On which will the most effort be concentrated?

Where will investments be made?

How will quality and cost be controlled? Measures? Incentives? Rewards?

What results will be expected versus competition in terms of:

Quality of service? Cost profile? Productivity? Morale/loyalty of servers?

Strategy/System Integration

To what extent are the strategy and delivery system internally consistent?

Can needs of the strategy be met by the delivery system?

If not, what changes must be made in:

The operating strategy? The service delivery system?

To what extent does the coordination of operating strategy and service delivery system insure:

High quality? High productivity? Low cost? High morale and loyalty of servers?

To what extent does this integration provide barriers to entry to competition?

Service Delivery System

What are important features of the service delivery system, including: The role of people? Technology? Equipment? Layout? Procedures?

What capacity does it provide? Normally? At peak levels?

To what extent does it: Help insure quality standards? Differentiate the service from competition? Provide barriers to entry by competitors?

Basic Element

Integrative Element

POSITIONING

The process of positioning follows naturally from identification of a market target that competitors also seek to serve. Firms that have most successfully positioned themselves have spent some time answering these questions: What is good service in the eyes of customers comprising the segment? To what extent do competitors provide it? Does the proposed service concept provide it? To the extent that customer expectations are never or rarely met, what steps must be taken to bring expectations into line with server capabilities, and vice versa?

THE "THREE Cs"

The company, the customer, and the competitor: How do they relate to one another on dimensions considered important to the customer? The objective of positioning is often to differentiate one product or service from another, either in the eyes of the customer, or in fact, or both. I use "differentiate" in the everyday sense of "develop distinguishing characteristics." Differentiation may be achieved either in terms of cost or product features, as diagrammed in Figure 2-2.

Many people, including bankers, regard lending as a business in which one loan is differentiated from another on the basis of small price differences by customers who often exhibit little long-term loyalty to a business lender. Others, who have taken the trouble to find out, have concluded that any service can be differentiated on nonprice bases.

"Universal Bank" need not despair of losing business to its lower-priced competitor, "Continental Bank," if it knows that the prospective borrower, "Automatic Hoist," values one or more elements of service design over low cost. For example, Automatic Hoist may be willing to pay more to avail itself of Universal's reputation for making funds available even in times of tight credit. How does Universal Bank's management learn of such needs? Through customer contact and informal or formal marketing research.

POSITIONING AND MARKETING RESEARCH

Effective positioning requires marketing research, something foreign to nearly all but the best-managed service firms. It is more complicated to research reactions to a service than to a product,

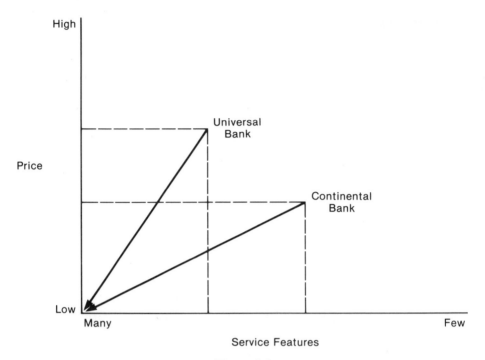

Figure 2-2
Positioning of Two Banks in Relation to a Borrower

especially for services in the developmental stage. Customers find it more difficult to put themselves into the role of using a prospective service than of using a product they can hold and see. This requires the testing of concepts as opposed to products. For example, one entrepreneur was able to gauge prospective demand for a luxury airline passenger service by showing pictures of aircraft interiors, describing service features, and asking prospective customers whether they would subscribe to membership in the service at rates reflecting varying multiples of existing first-class rates over the proposed routes.

When customers are familiar with services already in existence, measures of the various components of good service and of the extent to which competitors provide them can be more easily obtained. One of the regional telephone companies, in preparing for industry deregulation, learned from its major business users that some firms that used phone lines for data-processing purposes were interested in contracts providing 24-hour repair service, while retailers that were heavily dependent on phone service only during business hours wanted a guaranteed minimum-response-time for service interruptions only during those hours. In the past, the company offered a single service contract that treated all business customers alike. Company management concluded that it ran the risk of losing business to competitors who tailored their telephone services to specific industries' needs.

Christopher Lovelock has suggested that customer loyalty may not be gained by providing the most important dimensions of good service, because all competitors meet these requirements.[3] Secondary factors that affect market differentiation and customer decision making must, therefore, be identified. If competing airlines all offer safe service and identical schedules, ground or on-board service differences may take on added importance.

MAPPING COMPETITIVE STRENGTHS AND WEAKNESSES

The mapping of competitive positioning may offer an effective way of communicating the results of research or the goals of a company's strategy. When Southwest Airlines, one of the most successful airlines in recent years, entered competition against Braniff Airlines on routes within the state of Texas in 1971, it had the "map" in Figure 2-3 prepared.[4] This simple diagram conveys a great deal of information about two ways in which Southwest could differentiate its advertising from Braniff after it had satisfied the basic needs of its target market segment—business travelers—for schedules, available seats, and dependable arrivals.

The map suggests that Southwest's advertising could be differentiated to the degree it communicated either "fun" or "conservative" themes, in either obvious or subtle ways, to prospective travelers. While Braniff's advertising had been perceived as obvious and fun in earlier times when it had been the first to paint its planes designer colors and dress its flight attendants in uniforms by Gucci, its advertising was considered to have become more subtle and conservative. Southwest successfully seized the positioning opportunity: it promoted its new service around the theme of love. Service would originate from conveniently located Love Field in Dallas; flight attendants would wear shorts; love potions instead of drinks would be offered on board; and there would be

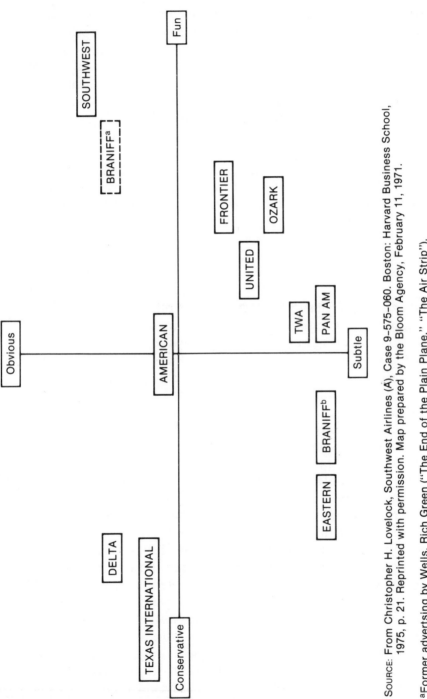

Source: From Christopher H. Lovelock, Southwest Airlines (A), Case 9-575-060. Boston: Harvard Business School, 1975, p. 21. Reprinted with permission. Map prepared by the Bloom Agency, February 11, 1971.

[a]Former advertising by Wells, Rich Green ("The End of the Plain Plane," "The Air Strip").

[b]Clinton Frank advertising.

Figure 2-3

A "Map" Employed by Southwest Airlines in the Initial Competitive Positioning
of its Advertising

love machines instead of ticketing machines. The company was also able to represent itself successfully as an upstart carrier that, unlike its "giant" competitor, cared for its customers in a market segment to which these appeals apparently made a difference.

The mapping process provided an effective way for Southwest's management to keep its major positioning goals in mind. Other service firms developing more complex positioning strategies have described them with two or more such maps.

ALIGNING CUSTOMER EXPECTATIONS AND SERVICE CAPABILITIES

Some service firms have found that customers judge services received in terms of the relation between perceived quality and expected quality. It is quite possible that relationships similar to those shown in Figure 2-4 exist for many services. If a service is

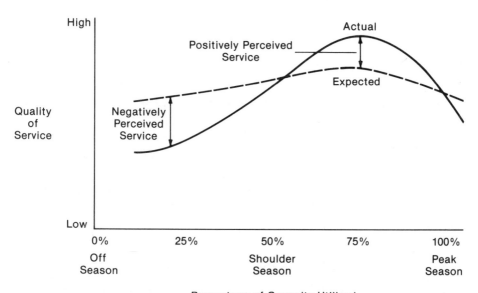

aThe curves shown here are based on general experience and are not fully documented by research.

Figure 2-4
Relationships Between Capacity Utilization and Actual, Expected, and
Perceived Quality of Service

regarded as good in the eyes of a manager but does not measure up to a customer's expectations, it will be rated as poor. Again, the difficult problem of how to measure customer expectations emerges because most customers cannot always articulate their expectations reliably.

Focus groups involving intensive discussions with valued customers or with randomly selected respondents from a targeted segment of the market have been employed for this purpose. Major business customers can of course be surveyed in some depth, but while companies or individuals may be able to rank the importance of various needs, they are often unable to supply information that would allow a server to calibrate the service delivered in relation to expectations on important service dimensions.

Instead of asking people what they expect, one leading airline measures the actual service that people receive, then asks them to evaluate it. By relating these two measures, it can adjust its service levels to meet most customers' perceptions of acceptable service. The same airline was one of the first to adopt a single queueing system in which all counters are served from one master line. The single queue reduces differences in the amount of time spent in line and guards against the phenomenon that "the other line always moves faster." While this approach does not provide for the customer with unusually high expectations, it enables firms in service retailing, including banks and airlines, to meet most customers' expectations at reasonable cost.[5]

Once a firm has set out to differentiate its service on the basis of unusually high quality, it may seek to raise customers' expectations through advertising and other educational activities, which puts the more conventional competitors at a disadvantage. This works, of course, only when customers regard such service improvements as important.

LEVERAGING VALUE OVER COST

A properly positioned service concept has to be provided at a margin that allows for adequate employee salaries, investment, and return on investment. The service concept and the operating strategy must therefore be designed so that the perceived value of a service in the eyes of a customer is sufficiently greater than the actual cost of supplying the service.

How do successful service firms "leverage" their activities to create what consulting firms call a "multiple" between price and cost so vital to long-run profit? Among the more important ways are standardizing, customizing, and emphasizing easily leveraged services; managing demand and supply; managing quality at critical points in a process; involving the customer in the delivery of the service; and the effective use of data.

COMBINING STANDARDIZED AND CUSTOMIZED ELEMENTS

Each of the policies most life insurance companies offer—straight life, term, variable annuity, and the like—is designed to meet a different set of customer needs. The life insurance salesperson, if effective, then tailors an insurance program to the needs of an individual customer by recommending policies selected from the standard building blocks the insurer offers.

In recent years, growing numbers of successful financial advisory services have taken a step further by recommending tailor-made financial programs fashioned from available, standardized investment opportunities, insurance policies, and trust vehicles for individual clients.

The customer may provide the customization. A vacation built from several standard elements may be devised to meet the specific needs of an individual. Increasingly, travelers are buying standard tour packages for their economy but also making provisions for leaving the tour at certain points to engage in activities that meet a particular interest. The "fly-drive" package that includes a rental car at destination has been designed successfully to meet this kind of need at a reasonable price.

EMPHASIZING EASILY LEVERAGED SERVICES

Some services are more easily leveraged than others. An automobile mechanic may find it difficult to earn a good margin on a complex repair job requiring the same combination of careful diagnosis, expert work, and luck required of a medical practitioner. On the other hand, a car wash costs very little, and everyone knows that a freshly washed car looks better, feels better, and even drives better than a dirty one. A combination of low- and high-leverage auto services can add up to a high level of customer satisfaction and a reasonable average margin.

One of the most successful of all service companies is Schlumberger, Ltd., whose major business, wireline logging, helps oil companies assess the likely success of oil drilling activities through the use of electronics and analytic procedures. Although the company has expanded far beyond this basic service, its wireline service alone produced a profit of about 30 percent on its $2.7 billion revenues in 1981. There are many reasons for Schlumberger's profits on sales being greater than any industrial company in the world. First, the company emphasizes the development and application of state-of-the-art technology and a worldwide network of the best geological engineers (the company has hired roughly 1 percent of all U.S. engineering graduates in recent years) in providing a service that holds a 70 percent market share in its industry.

Schlumberger's wireline service is also immensely valuable to petroleum explorers, enabling them to save hundreds of thousands of dollars on each dry hole investment that they can avoid or minimize. And even with its regularly increased prices, Schlumberger's fees represent no more than 2 to 5 percent of a customer's drilling cost. But this small fee provides considerable room for leverage and helps account for the fact that for some time the company has been able to price its services at twice its costs.[6]

MANAGING DEMAND AND SUPPLY

Customers rarely enjoy intended service levels at periods of peak demand. A lending officer may not respond as rapidly as desired. A retail clerk is overworked at precisely the time that business potential is greatest. And even the gas burner on the kitchen stove may not provide the proper intensity of heat when all the burners are being used.

Conversely, service firms have trouble achieving intended levels of cost and productivity during slack periods of demand, especially firms with labor-intensive services that are not able to reduce staffing levels at such times. A "reverse demand-service curve" takes effect in such services as retailing and in-flight airline operations, where slack demand contributes to employee boredom—a psychological tendency to let down in serving customers—and a poorer-than-planned service level.

Across the broad spectrum of services, many are operated most effectively at an average rate of no more than 75 percent of theoretical capacity. At this rate the intended level of service can be provided a good share of the time. Where possible, of course, both

demand and supply can be managed to realize the desired relationship. The leveraging of value and cost of service takes place
through this process.

Services requiring a commitment to a given level of capacity far
in advance of actual demand may have little choice but to try to
maximize value and cost differences by managing demand. Thus,
an airline management that "sizes" its fleet every six months is
locked into a certain level of capacity, including equipment and
staffing. An electric utility sizes its capacity further in advance of
demand, and it must size to a higher proportion of its expected
peak than the airline, given the critical nature of its services. Once
such basic decisions have been made, both must concentrate on
managing demand through off-peak price incentives, service arrangements restricted to off-peak periods, and similar induce-
ments. At the very least, an attempt may be made to shift demand
to the "shoulder" season (see Figure 2-4). When such demand can
be shifted all the way to the slack period, not only is even greater
economic leverage realized but the quality of service during the
former slack period may actually be improved.

Other firms in similar circumstances may try to engage in value-
enhancing service activities that can be postponed until off-peak
periods. American Home Shield, which offers contracts to
homeowners for servicing heating, plumbing, electrical, and other
facilities in the home, concentrates on scheduling annual inspections at a time when seasonal peaks for emergency calls, such as
those for furnace maintenance in the coldest winter months, are
not expected.

Services for which demand can be "chased" with varying staffing levels are those in which management is focused on supply.
Here, the accurate forecasting and the identification of regular variations in demand become most important, if not always possible.
As Sasser has pointed out, a chase strategy requires that flexibility
be preserved in managing both human resources and equipment.
This strategy often argues for the use of short-term or part-time
employees with the attendant high rate of turnover and high training costs, especially for jobs requiring lower skill levels.[7] Advo-
cates of chase strategies for managing supply may be more likely to
lease or rent as opposed to buying certain types of equipment or
buildings.

The most successful service firms analyze the character of the demand for their services and the ways of meeting it, and then they build operating strategies designed to manage one or the other or both. This may require flexibility in equipping or staffing for various service levels, or the willingness to forego certain business. Such firms pay a great deal of attention to the resultant trade-offs in revenues and costs.

QUALITY CONTROL

The difficulty of achieving consistently high quality is stressed as a major difference between managing a service firm and managing a product-manufacturing firm by those who have done both.[8] The difficulty of controlling quality holds particularly for services involving a high level of direct contact between server employees and customers. And yet those firms that have been able to achieve consistent quality not only set themselves apart from their competition, they often create services with high value that offer unusually high margins from a highly loyal customer base. They have discovered many things that have eluded their competitors. For example, among the most effective forms of quality control are those that tap an individual's inner desire to provide good service—as opposed to those solutions that merely throw more supervision at a problem.

The Marriott Corporation and Delta Airlines pay particular attention to employee training, involvement, incentives, and in some cases, ownership. Management often is on a first-name basis. Employees are featured in their ads. Internal communications are as important as those with customers, and they range from personal attention to contests and company newspapers, all communicating the company's purpose and its high standards of service and building employee pride in meeting them. Such positive approaches, however, are complex and involve many internally consistent elements practiced by people who sincerely believe in them and care for the people they are managing. Such approaches also take time. Most often they are developed as part of an operating strategy designed in conjunction with the service concept.

Supervision as a means of controlling quality may take many forms. At one leading secretarial school, students are passed from one short instructional module, taught by one faculty member, to another. The second instructor depends on the first to have taught certain skills and concepts. Knowing this, the first instructor feels some pressure to make sure the material is covered and understood. Similarly, at Shouldice Hospital supervision of doctors is mainly by peers.

Where the operating strategy calls for a highly visible service delivery process, employees may respond to being visually exposed to customers by exercising more self-control when providing a service. The piece of silverware dropped on the floor of the restaurant is more likely to be put into the dirty silverware container than one dropped in the kitchen. Such visibility affects matters as diverse as adherence to dress codes and the manner in which the customer's belongings—luggage or valet-parked car—are handled.

INVOLVING THE CUSTOMER

With a carefully planned company-operating strategy, customers can be subtly involved not only in the control of service quality but also in the delivery of the service itself. Levitz built a strategy of furniture retailing around low prices and low costs made possible by customers' willingness to drive to the stores, accept furniture in crates, and even transport their purchases home and assemble them themselves. This strategy saved Levitz a great deal of transport effort and also shifted liability to the customer for commonly experienced damage in the delivery process.

Self-service in all its forms, ranging in fast-food restaurants from drive-in pick-up to preparation (adding condiments) to table cleanup, represents customer involvement in the service delivery process. It is usually justified in customers' minds by cost and time savings (direct telephone dialing), accessibility (24-hour automatic bank teller machines), impersonality (self-ticketing and rental auto turn-in procedures), and accuracy (salad bar selections). Whatever their form, such efforts have not been successful without some form of justification important to customers.

EFFECTIVE USE OF DATA

An operating strategy designed to make effective use of the large quantities of data flowing into many service firms can enhance service and reduce costs at the same time. Heating-oil retailers can time deliveries during winter months by combining data about each customer's last delivery, storage tank size, and historical usage rate or house size with the computation of the number of degree days of weather experienced at different temperatures. If the retailer uses these data properly, customers can fully rely on the availability of heating oil without excessive delivery costs for the retailer.

A credit card service builds expenditure profiles for its customers; broken patterns may signal potential problems, such as a stolen card. If such expenditures are sufficiently large and are being made long distances from the cardholder's address, one major travel card issuer will attempt to verify whether the cardholder is indeed traveling in the area in which purchases are being made, instead of disallowing retailers' requests for charges.

INTEGRATING THE OPERATING STRATEGY AND THE SERVICE DELIVERY SYSTEM

At the Rural/Metro Fire Department, the service concept is effective low-cost fire protection targeted to growing suburban communities that are in the process of organizing their fire protection services under severe limitations on budgets for public services.[9] Rural/Metro differentiates its approach away from traditional fire protection by avoiding the general tendencies to overstaff, to buy oversized equipment, and to provide uneconomic levels of protection.

Rural/Metro's operating strategy provides good service at low cost by analyzing a community's needs and then designing staffing levels and equipment to meet exactly those needs. Several years ago the company carefully reviewed fire data and discovered that nearly 80 percent of fires were extinguished with no more than 300 gallons of water, a fraction of the quantity delivered by large, expensive pumpers. With this knowledge, Rural/Metro was able to respond with a service delivery system involving equipment of its own design. Its "attack truck" is a pick-up truck painted lime green (to reduce night-time rear-end accidents) and outfitted with a 300-gallon tank that is operable by a single firefighter, thus reducing both investment and operating costs. The same approach was used with fire hoses. Data collected from tests indicated that a basic problem in firefighting is being unable to deliver enough water quickly to smother a fire in its early stages. Rural/Metro reacted by ordering hoses four inches in diameter rather than the more traditional two-and-a-half-inch diameter ones. Improvement was dramatic.

The company has logged data on various buildings in its community so that when it receives a fire call to a particular address, it can send equipment suitable to the structure, avoiding the overkill often produced by equipment of standard design employed universally by traditionally managed fire departments. It has even experimented with microfilm viewers mounted in its trucks to provide information about the floor plans of selected buildings, thus permitting the study of the fire site by firefighters en route.

Perhaps the most important element of integration between Rural/Metro's operating strategy and its service delivery system is its personnel policy. The company's research suggested that the typical firefighter spent no more than 10 percent of duty hours in training, in maintaining essential equipment and facilities, and in actual firefighting. By developing agreements with one local city government to employ city employees on an as-needed, part-time basis, Rural/Metro was able to cut its full-time personnel roster to 20 percent of other departments its size.

The overall results of this effort have been significantly higher-than-average fire protection to the community at less than half the cost incurred by other communities comparable in size and characteristics. It has achieved high labor productivity with higher-than-average wages for typical city employees, and a reasonable profit for Rural/Metro.

The power of a systematically conceived and targeted service concept, supported by an operating strategy that provides effective value-cost differentiation and by a service delivery system integrated with the strategy, is illustrated once again.

The linkage between operating strategy and service delivery systems can be evaluated by applying criteria shown in Figure 2-1 as part of the overall scheme of basic and integrative elements of a strategic service vision. Certain questions posed in Figure 2-1 have not yet been addressed. Others have been touched on but warrant further attention. The first of these is the matter of positioning.

CHAPTER THREE

Positioning in Competitive Service Strategies

The most successful service firms separate themselves from "the pack" to achieve a distinctive position in relation to their competitors. They differentiate themselves from their competition by altering typical characteristics of their respective industries to their competitive advantage. This produces either improved service or reduced cost or both. The results speak for themselves. Consider the following examples.

In the traditional retail establishment, sales are made "on-line," with the salesperson in direct contact with the customer. Catalog retailers, who have enjoyed rapid growth in recent years, have eliminated the direct contact, thereby appealing to self-assured customers seeking lower prices while reducing personnel costs substantially. And more recently, firms such as Comp-U-Card have introduced services whereby customers can order a wide variety of well-known durable goods through their personal computers or by telephone at discounts even greater than those offered by catalog retailers, discounts approximating 40 percent to 50 percent off suggested retail prices. The discounts are made possible by the elimination not only of salespeople and typical retailing facilities but of printed catalogs, which often become dated soon after publication. Comp-U-Card's electronic catalog in one recent period was being updated at the rate of 50,000 changes per month.

Comp-U-Card substitutes for the traditional catalog retail store a process called Comp-U-Store, in which customers can scan or ask an operator to scan a frequently-updated electronic catalog, make purchases, and pay for them by communicating their credit card numbers by telephone or computer. The surprise is not that Comp-U-Card has discovered a group of self-assured, innovative shoppers but that the company found so many—about 1.8 million as of one recent count. As a result, its sales of more than 100,000 different items yielded commissions of more than $28 million to Comp-U-Card in 1984, a figure growing about as rapidly as the company's compounded growth rate in sales of roughly 250 percent in the last three years.

The Forum Corporation offers a range of consulting services, many of them associated with improving the quality of supervision in large organizations. In an industry as people-intensive as any, this company has sponsored the development of a number of devices that yield data about individual management practices. This information can be fed back to the individual in computer-prepared evaluations written in report form that would require hours of interpretation and writing if done in the more typical consulting manner. These reports, supplemented by person-to-person consultation, save many hours of personal effort by substituting software in which The Forum Corporation has made substantial capital investments. In so doing, it has made a people-intensive process more capital-intensive.

When faced with McDonald's, a competitor with a highly standardized product and service, Burger King told each prospective customer to "have it your way" by attempting to customize certain elements of the fast-food process it offered. By accomplishing this through the use of a wider variety of condiments applied to customer specification, Burger King was able to offer an alternative at a price not much higher than McDonald's and establish a position as a strong number two to its largest rival.

In each of these cases, one company set itself apart competitively by converting a possible industry disadvantage to its own advantage. This pattern characterizes many of the most successful strategies found in the service industries.

BASIC COMPETITIVE STRATEGIES

Michael Porter has argued persuasively that there are three generic competitive strategies: overall cost leadership, differentiation, and focus.[1] This first of these can yield high profits through low prices, high sales volume, and high market share. The second should foster high prices, margins, and profits with a much smaller sales volume and share of market. The third may include a combination of low costs and some differentiation designed to appeal to members of a highly focused market niche. A firm achieving both low costs and high product differentiation should be in a position to dominate a market as few firms can today. A firm able to achieve neither is a firm in a difficult, if not impossible, competitive situation if it is not able to address its offerings to a well-focused market niche not well served by its competitors.

Achieving distance from the pack may lead to lower cost; at other times the result is service differentiation. Some elements of strategy may contribute both to lower cost and more highly differentiated services. Many of these are shown in Figure 3-1. The most

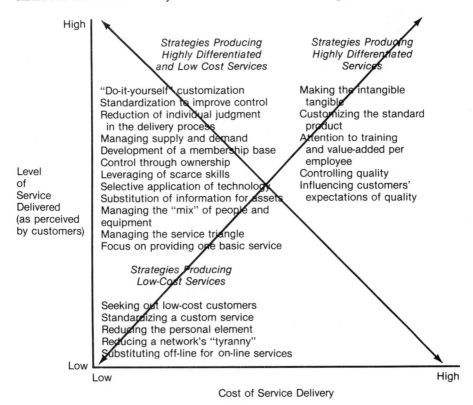

Figure 3-1
Typical Effects of Alternative Strategic Departures in the Service Industries

successful service firms understand the relationship in Figure 3-1 all too well and provide excellent examples for others.

STRATEGIC DEPARTURES THAT REDUCE COST

Firms in various service industries have sought lower costs by seeking out low-cost customers, standardizing a custom service, eliminating some of the personal element in service delivery, reducing the "tyranny" of the network, and substituting an "off-line" service for one previously delivered "on-line."

SEEKING OUT LOW-COST CUSTOMERS

Some customers cost less to serve than others, without any deterioration in the perceived level of service delivered. Some firms have built their strategies around this principle. In the life insurance industry, people who do not pilot airplanes, smoke, or ride motorcycles are eligible for lower rates than those who do. The customers represent lower risk and therefore produce lower costs.

At Dr. Shouldice's hernia hospital near Toronto, described earlier, patients are screened carefully. Only those in good physical condition are accepted, and those with forms of hernia other than the one in which the hospital specializes are turned away. All this contributes to rapid rates of recovery and of discharge, reflected in both Shouldice's costs and prices.

Other customers are low-cost because they are willing to do part of the work of producing or delivering a service. Supermarket shoppers spend time and money to drive beyond the corner grocery store, inform themselves about various products, and transport their purchases home. The success of more recently developed warehouse stores requiring even more customer effort attests to the importance of such customers.

Still other customers represent low-cost market segments because they are willing to have their demand managed. Companies selling by appointment, restaurants operated on a reservation-only policy, and utility customers willing to limit their peak-time usage of electricity are examples.

STANDARDIZING A CUSTOM SERVICE

Hyatt Legal Services has been able to provide very low-cost legal counsel. In an industry requiring highly customized services, this company has identified a middle-income segment of the population with relatively simple legal needs for wills, uncontested divorces, adoptions, and bankruptcies. It provides a relatively standardized service at modest cost in storefront facilities that are less intimidating to those with little experience in obtaining legal services. Hyatt prospers through standardization of a process fraught with uncertainty about effectiveness and costs.

To the extent that a service can be standardized, management can market its characteristics and the results that customers can expect. A life insurer specifies exactly the services to be delivered to a policy-holder and can market these features. In many of Holiday Inn's motels a frequent traveler, often on business, becomes familiar with the standard designs of rooms and fixtures and counts on them. Holiday Inn features this advantage in its ads and at the same time achieves lower costs and prices.

REDUCING THE PERSONAL ELEMENT IN SERVICE DELIVERY

Many firms have proceeded cautiously to find out just how much of the personal element can or should be eliminated and have ultimately prospered using this potentially high-risk strategy.

Perhaps the most pervasive example at present is the introduction of automatic teller machines (ATMs) by an increasing number of banks. Aside from their other features, these machines in many locations make it unnecessary for the customer to enter a bank, let alone interact with an employee. With increasing levels of usage, ATMs are greatly reducing costs per transaction in many banks.

At what point can this strategy work to the firm's disadvantage? Mark Twain Bancshares, the highly successful St. Louis-based bank, focuses its efforts on providing personal banking and related services to individuals with annual incomes of $50,000 or more. It has foregone the development of an extensive ATM network. The country's largest bank, Citibank (a subsidiary of Citicorp), has hedged its bets by opening three different types of outlets: ATMs at one extreme, limited service branches capable of processing the most simple transactions for those wishing to deal face-to-face with their banker teller, and full-service branches at which the more complex (and often highly profitable) needs of customers can be served by experts. In reducing the personal element in services, whether health care or financial or travel services, people delivering the service must understand the importance of what they do from both a marketing and an operational standpoint.

Firms seeking lower costs may reduce both the custom and the

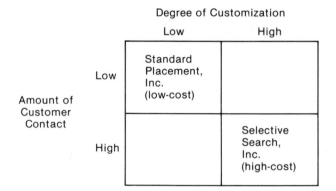

Figure 3-2
The Positioning of Two Executive Placement Firms: Relationships Between
Customization and Contact in the Service Delivery Process

human content of their services. David Maister and Christopher Lovelock have developed a structure for considering these factors so that competitive alternatives within individual service industries can be identified. They have arrayed the degree of customization associated with a company's service against the amount of customer contact required of the individual service provider.[2] The relationships are shown in Figure 3-2.

"Standard Placement, Inc.," an executive placement firm, may concentrate on volume of activity merely by making available résumés of candidates for a job. Whatever customization may be involved is provided by the client; contact between the customer and the service deliverer is limited; and the amount of judgment exercised by the latter is small. "Selective Search," in contrast, establishes through interview with the client the requirements for the job, sorts available people, and introduces to the client those few candidates who may best meet the needs of the position.

The first approach may allow the use of service providers of lower skill at lower salary and with less training. The low cost to those clients able and willing to inject large quantities of their own judgment into the process may be its major benefit. The second approach is likely to be much more costly, of interest to clients who possess little expertise or who may want to shift responsibility for much of the work to an outside firm. Both strategies may be pursued successfully by placement firms if employee selection, compensation, and training policies as well as marketing efforts are carefully designed.

REDUCING A NETWORK'S TYRANNY

Whether networks consist of telephone exchanges connected by wire or retail outlets and travelers connected by a common credit card, they cost a great deal of money to develop. Because certain portions of them are fixed in place geographically, they often require a highly disciplined management to ensure that demand is generated that can serve the network at reasonable cost. Firms able to reduce this network "tyranny" have set themselves apart in performance.

Utilities confront this phenomenon as much as any group of service firms, as the profit models for several groups of service firms show in Table 3-1. The large investment in utility networks is reflected there in a low .43 ratio of revenues to assets, caused by a large asset base. However, individual utilities may not encounter the problem. Texas Eastern turns over its assets three times as fast as Commonwealth Edison, as shown in Column 7 of Table 3-1. Texas Eastern is able to limit its investment and reduce the tyranny of the network because it distributes its gas to a limited number of retailers. Consequently, its network is much less complex than that of Commonwealth Edison, which also retails its power. Serving individual homes as well as industry, Commonwealth Edison derives less revenue in relation to its assets.

When Federal Express entered the air package delivery business, it was faced with a substantial investment in a network before it could begin serving the public. Even though the business required the largest capital venture in history up to that time, the company reduced the investment by designing an air transport network in which no packages were flown directly from origin to destination. By flying everything to a central sorting hub and back out again, Federal Express greatly reduced the tyranny of the network. Each time it adds a city to its network, it simply adds one more route to the hub rather than adding as many routes as cities served, a problem often confronted by other airlines.

The efficiency of this strategy is underscored by the fact that several major passenger airline operators have also begun to develop hubs, for this and other reasons.

Table 3–1
Contrasting Profit Models for Selected Companies in the U.S. Service Industries, 1984[a]

	"Profit Models" by Firm and Industry							Company and Industry Profit Model						
Company or Industry	(1) Revenues	(2) Assets	(3) Net Income per firm	(4) Equity	(5) Employees per Firm	(6) Revenues/ Employee	(7) Revenues/ Assets	x	(8) Net Income/ Revenues	x	(9) Assets/ Equity	=	(10) Net Income/ Equity
	(millions of dollars per firm)												
Two Utilities:													
Commonwealth Edison	4,930	14,713	875	5,514	18,400	$267,900	.34	x	17.75%	x	2.67	=	16.11%
Texas Eastern	6,194	5,757	212	1,538	14,700	421,400	1.08	x	3.42	x	3.74	=	13.81
Average for the 50 largest utilities	4,037	9,331	452	3,335	25,600	157,700	.43	x	11.20	x	2.80	=	13.48
Two Transportation Companies:													
Federal Express	1,436	1,526	115	718	18,400	78,100	.94	x	8.00	x	2.13	=	16.02
Allied Van Lines	516	76	8	29	965	534,700	6.79	x	1.55	x	2.62	=	27.57
Average for the 50 largest transportation companies	2,141	2,358	118	849	19,400	110,400	.91	x	5.51	x	2.78	=	13.94
Two Diversified Service Companies:													
Hospital Corp. of America	3,499	4,829	297	1,870	79,000	44,300	.72	x	8.49	x	2.58	=	15.77
Service Master Industries	850	103	30	68	7,400	114,900	8.25	x	3.53	x	1.51	=	43.97
Average for 90 of the 100 largest diversified service companies[b]	2,107	1,955	61	530	17,500	120,400	1.08	x	2.90	x	3.69	=	11.56
Weighted average for 454 of the largest 500 service companies[a]	2,584	7,564	124	1,008	20,100	128,400	.34	x	4.79	x	7.50	=	12.21
Weighted average for 485 of the largest 500 manufacturing companies[c]	3,589	2,895	179	1,310	28,600	125,500	1.24	x	4.99	x	2.21	=	13.67

[a]Source: "The Fortune Service 500," *Fortune*, June 10, 1985, pp. 175–195. The weighted average for all service industries excludes 46 of the largest 500; 25 are mutual insurance companies, seven are stock insurance companies not breaking out equity, three are subsidiaries of foreign banks, and eleven are cooperatives or others not reporting profits. Numbers are rounded. © 1985 Time Inc. All rights reserved.

[b]Averages do not include performance figures for ten firms operated as cooperatives, for which comparable profit figures are not available.

[c]Source: "The 500," *Fortune*, April 29, 1985, pp. 265–285. Fifteen companies' results are not included either because they are cooperatives and do not report net income or because they do not publish comparable information. Numbers are rounded. © 1985 Time Inc. All rights reserved.

Brokerage businesses, matching buyers and sellers for a fee, often are faced with a form of network tyranny. They encounter unusual start-up costs as they construct their base of buyers and sellers and establish their information communications network. Whether in real estate, finance, or international barter, the effectiveness of a broker depends on the number of appropriately qualified buyers and sellers maintained in its data base. The rate at which a broker successfully brings buyers and sellers together increases with the number of each with whom the broker can establish relationships.

Improvements in communications technology have facilitated brokerage-based strategies. Century 21 Real Estate Corporation can provide a frequently updated listing of homes nationwide to its 6,400 affiliated individual brokers. Franchises of this organization, the largest of its kind, collectively brokered 11 percent of all U.S. home sales in 1983.[3]

TAKING SERVICE OPERATIONS "OFF-LINE"

Some services are inherently "on-line," defying anyone to divorce the server from the customer. Hair (other than a wig) must be styled "on-line"; passenger transportation is delivered "on-line." Some of the faster growing services can be "decoupled" and produced with a significant "off-line" content: data-based services that can be accessed by personal computers, catalog as opposed to more conventional retailing services, and freight transportation.[4]

From an operating standpoint the relative desirability of providing services "off-line" or "on-line" is a subject of debate. The predominant view is that economies are more likely, skills can be more easily leveraged, and quality is easier to control if the service can be performed "off-line": out of sight of the customer and even at a location other than that of the customer.[5] Customer contacts handled by mail can be more easily monitored and controlled than those conducted in person. The order-filling staff at a catalog retailer's warehouse can be more closely supervised than a sales staff in a department store. More attention can be focused on getting the order filled than on aspects of personal appearance and manner that often are of equal importance in an "on-line" service, aspects that often cost more money and require higher levels of skills among servers.

STRATEGIC DEPARTURES THAT ENHANCE SERVICE

Firms basing their strategies on service differentiation have devoted considerable effort to introducing tangible features into typically intangible services, customizing generally standardized services, training those who will be interacting personally with
customers, influencing quality expectations, and controlling quality. A differentiated service is thus achieved at higher costs but the
targeted customer is more than willing to pay them.

MAKING THE INTANGIBLE TANGIBLE

How do you sell an intangible to a customer? By making it more
tangible, according to Theodore Levitt.[6] The written insurance policy, its attractive appearance, and the clarity of its language help
make the service more tangible. Trouble-shooting services such as
those associated with home maintenance may employ annual inspections or periodically mailed "advisories" to subscribers. A
hotel may place collars with the word "sanitized" on its toilets. A
travel agent may send roses to the secretaries of its best clients. Or
Merrill Lynch, providing relatively intangible financial services
(intangible, at least, to those who have not used them) will associate itself with a symbol meaningful for investors: a bull.

Services with extensive real estate or equipment offer a wider
range of opportunity for image-building to attract first-time purchasers and influence regular users. Color schemes, uniforms, the
appearance of buildings, and the use of logos and signs are some of
many ways in which the intangible is made tangible.

Good service often leaves no trail. In the building maintenance
and cleaning service industry, the best work goes unnoticed. Poor
quality work, however, when noticed, often leads to a change of
suppliers. The cleaning service industry might thereby seem to be
one of the least attractive to investors, yet the company producing
the highest return on stockholders' equity in the *Fortune* 100
largest diversified service companies between 1973 and 1983 was
ServiceMaster Industries, which provides housekeeping and other
services to hospitals, schools, and corporations.[7] As part of its regular service, ServiceMaster provides advice on repairs needed, pre-
ventive maintenance that a client should consider, and regular
inspections with building managers, all highly visible aspects of an
intangible service.

Leonard Berry suggests that services are made "more palpable by creating a tangible representation of it."[8] The bank credit card is one example. Other firms have associated their services with objects or images through their advertising programs. The following slogans are all intended to create "tangible images" of what intangible insurance can provide:

> "You are in good *hands* with Allstate."
> "I've got a piece of the *Rock*."
> "Under the Travelers *umbrella*."
> "The Nationwide *blanket* of protection."[9]

CUSTOMIZING THE STANDARD PRODUCT

Enhancing quality usually requires an understanding of customer needs, whether for satisfaction of vanity or for more tangible needs. Customization need cost very little. The hotel operator able to address a resident by name has taken little extra time to achieve what may be a significantly raised level of service to some customers. In our earlier example, Burger King's management correctly perceived that while McDonald's low prices and generally good quality appealed to many people, its standardized products repelled or bored others who were willing to pay a bit more at Burger King to enjoy a more highly customized food service.

ATTENTION TO TRAINING AND VALUE ADDED
PER EMPLOYEE

The amount of value added per employee influences the way in which the "human resource wheel" is managed in a service firm. If a firm supplies professional consulting services, the value added by its employees, who are often partners and associates, consists of nearly all the fees the firm earns. The value added is high because of the value placed on the firm's services by its clients, which results directly from the high level of skill of the consultants.

As shown in Figure 3-3, high "value added" makes possible (and in turn is made possible by) high levels of compensation and significant investments in personal development, which can lead to increased employee satisfaction, lower turnover, lower new-employee training costs, and higher value added per employee. This, of course, is what is possible if the "wheel" in Figure 3-3 turns clockwise. At times of reduced revenues or overutilization of the most skilled employees, actions to preserve or build profits can bring the wheel's clockwise movement to a halt. Once this occurs,

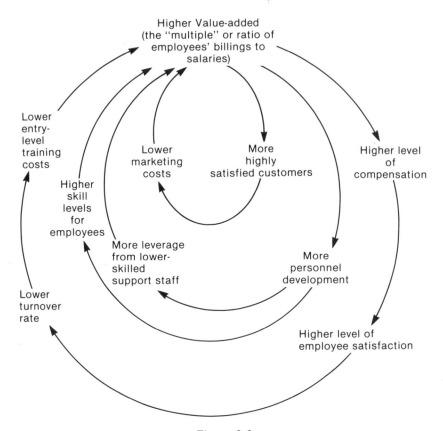

Figure 3-3
The Human Resource "Wheel" in People-intensive Services

it is difficult to begin the motion once again without significant investment of time and capital.

A service strategy centered on hard-to-replicate elements such as people is more difficult to emulate than one based on standard elements like readily available equipment. A "Singapore Girls" campaign carried on by Singapore Airlines involved much more than advertising the unique service provided by stewardesses and other employees. The program was backed up by extensive training and quality control, and it has been difficult to replicate for competitors who operate similar equipment on Far Eastern air travel routes.

Leading firms in their respective service industries are known among competitors for the quality of their personnel programs, including training. These companies place high priority on current investments in people that yield long-term returns. Many have spent years building a strategy based on enhanced service, and at times strong faith among managers has been needed to achieve the eventual payoff. Chapter 7 is entirely devoted to this important issue.

CONTROLLING QUALITY

Those who have managed in both product- and service-oriented firms repeatedly state that quality control in service firms presents the greater problem. The problem varies directly with the amount of individual judgment exercised by the server in delivering the service and with the difficulty of directly supervising the service transaction.[10]

Nonetheless, quality has been achieved in leading service firms through training, explicit procedures, technology, and peer and customer pressure as well as through direct supervision. For example, even though direct supervision is possible in Magic Pan's chain of restaurants, the company has relied on the design of foolproof machines to restrict employee judgment in producing what are generally regarded as excellent crepes used in many of the restaurant's offerings.

Other firms have emphasized job design. A chain of stores called Waffle House, operating mainly in the southern United States, relies on detailed job descriptions to guide employees through each day until procedures are internalized and the operation becomes self-controlling.

In circumstances where server judgment is important and the ability to provide direct supervision is limited, peer pressure is used. The publication of student ratings of instructors sensitive to their colleagues' perceptions of their teaching abilities can influence performance. Peer review by senior partners of the quality of work on a project-by-project basis in an architectural firm serves the same purpose.

Customers and the public in general can be enlisted in the effort. At Chemical Waste Management, Inc., the largest hauler of toxic waste in the United States, the company's phone number is painted prominently on each truck and the local manager's name and home address are displayed at each storage facility. These efforts are intended to provide control over quality as the company pursues an important goal of complying with the laws and with company operating standards in its transport and storage activities.

Effective training and motivation of the individual is the surest way of getting to the heart of quality control. Firms most successful in these efforts are those with strong institutional values often traceable to their founders. The consistently high level of quality enjoyed by customers at Disney entertainment facilities is a reflection of the care the company takes in training and motivating thousands of people each year, many of them seasonal or casual employees. From the first day's experience in a class called Traditions 1 to the use of "cast member" for employee and "on stage" for tasks involving customer contact, Disney trains its new people for "the show." Executives spend one week each year taking tickets or selling popcorn in an effort to maintain a high level of sensitivity to operational needs and problems. Even casual employees are made to feel part of the institution through frequent communication, positive feedback, and a full set of support facilities that customers never see.[11]

INFLUENCING QUALITY EXPECTATIONS

Several years ago a major automobile manufacturer undertook a study of customer perceptions of the quality of service provided by its dealers. The outcome was a shock: Its dealers not only trailed auto service centers operated by mass merchandisers such as Sears or Montgomery Ward, but operators of corner service stations led all types of auto service establishments in customer perceptions of quality.

The manufacturer then studied its dealers' customers' expectations in relation to their actual experiences. They found that customers took their toughest problems to their authorized auto dealers, with high expectations of having them resolved. Disappointments occurred sometimes. If the task involved changing the oil or repairing a tire, customers went to the corner service station. Disappointments were rare. The convergence of customer expectations and actual experiences led to a high rating for the corner station but a low rating for the authorized dealer.

The manufacturer then instituted several programs involving measurements and incentives to encourage dealers to give more attention to the quality of service delivered. It also launched a promotional program portraying the dealer's mechanic as an expert in his trade but sufficiently human not to know all the answers all the time.

What is good service? Clearly, its definition varies by customer and by transaction, but it is influenced as much by expectations as by experiences with services actually delivered.[12]

The ability to influence those expectations will vary inversely with the extent to which customers have defined their expectations. Of course, the firm seeking to improve perceptions of quality only by reducing expectations may be in for trouble from competition in the long term. But such efforts may usefully accompany a program of improved service that responds to customers' perceptions of their needs.

STRATEGIC DEPARTURES THAT REDUCE COST AND ENHANCE SERVICE

Competitive strategies often have the combined effects of both reducing cost and enhancing service. Examples of such strategies are provided by firms that rely on "do-it-yourself" customization, standardization leading to improved control, the reduction of individual judgment in the delivery process, the inventorying of service capacity as well as demand, development of a "membership" base, control through "ownership," leveraging of their most highly valued skills, selective application of technology, the substitution of assets with information, balancing people and relative assets, managing the service triangle, and focusing on a single level of service or type of customer.

"DO-IT-YOURSELF" CUSTOMIZATION

Since costs are reduced when customers provide their own services, service industries often intentionally involve the customer in the production process. AT&T encourages persons telephoning long distance to dial their own calls by offering price discounts and emphasizing the time-saving aspects of the practice, which also saves AT&T large sums of money. But customer involvement is not always planned. A flight attendant faced with serving a full meal on a short flight under favorable wind conditions may ask passengers to assist in disposing of their meal trays. Rarely are passengers unwilling to help.

Customers may consider "do-it-yourself" service preferable to traditional methods. The salad bar craze has simultaneously reduced costs of restaurant labor and increased customer satisfaction. Luxury hotels, faced with problems of providing room service for incidental but important items, such as ice, have sought solutions appropriate to their overall service strategy. Instead of installing ice machines in corridors of their hotels, they have invested in small "mini bars" for each room. Providing ice in this manner not only is suitable to a "luxury" image, but allows the customer to mix his or her favorite refreshment, removing a source of complaint for hotel managers who operate traditional room service and at the same time conserving cost.[13]

By the same token, attempts to engage customers in delivering a service have failed where they were not convinced of the benefits. The junk heap for such efforts contains the nine-digit mail code and customer reporting of utility meter readings in certain neighborhoods.

Since customization of services often increases their perceived value, letting customers "customize-it-yourself" reduces cost. Combining may enhance a service at lower cost. Thus, CompuServe offers a vast menu of information, communication, travel, and shopping services that can be used by its computer-owning subscribers. Each subscriber selects from the menu in much the same way that one selectively reads a newspaper, concentrating on the desired kinds of information. The customer customizes the service.

At H & R Block, this concept is a central element of its tax preparation service, embodied in the company's introduction some years ago of the Taxsaver, an envelope in which a taxpayer can file an entire year's receipts. According to a senior executive of the company:

> [The Taxsaver] serves two important functions. It not only helps organize our client's receipts, making our job easier and the tax preparer's time more productive at tax time, but it keeps the name of our company in full view of our customers 12 months a year. Our tax record books for business, farm, rental, and automobile expenses perform a similar function. We distribute millions of these items each year and, in a sense, it provides for some of our least expensive advertising.[14]

Customization through customer involvement has enabled each of these firms to deliver high-level service at reasonable cost. This is perhaps one reason why H & R Block found CompuServe a sufficiently attractive buy after a long search for a service-oriented company with a profit potential as great as its own.

STANDARDIZATION LEADING TO IMPROVED CONTROL

The management of Waffle House, a regional fast-food chain, has for years based its success in part on the fact that most of its small individual shops are standardized to allow for comparison and control. A supervisor for each region spends most of his time helping the least productive shop improve its operations. As a result, the company's costs as a proportion of total costs have a much smaller variance from one unit to another than many of its competitors operating units of varying design. In this case, standardization has led directly to improved control and service quality.

REDUCTION OF INDIVIDUAL JUDGMENT IN THE DELIVERY PROCESS

Service industries employ massive numbers of people, many of whom have limited education and skills. Hence, delivery systems providing good service at the level of customer contact in circumstances where supervision is limited must be developed carefully.

Waffle House, once again, uses detailed job descriptions listing hour-by-hour the tasks to be done by the two or three people staffing each store. The objective is to develop habit patterns for the performance of routine tasks so that employees' time is freed up to provide interaction with customers. Interaction often leads to higher sales per hour per store, an important Waffle House objective. Other organizations may rely on technology or work area layout to accomplish the same purpose, as in McDonald's approach to fast-food retailing.

Other firms have attempted to accomplish the same objective with close supervision. By and large, however, they have found this an expensive method and a poor use of supervision, which is more effectively used to train people how to use judgment in providing good service. Because jobs in services are delivered by persons with limited initial abilities the nature of hierarchy is changing. Although there may be less need for judgment at the first level of customer contact—in a hotel's telephone switchboard, say—judgment may be a highly desired quality in an assistant manager. But when a service organization promotes from within, how are potential managers to be selected from entry-level people? (The issue is explored in Chapter 7.)

MANAGING SUPPLY AND DEMAND

The capacity of a service firm is often difficult to measure, particularly if the firm relies on people and data more than on processes or equipment that require set times to accomplish various tasks.

Human beings rarely maintain the same level of productivity at all times. They often meet deadlines only by "superhuman" effort. And while it might be argued that this kind of effort should be unnecessary in a well-managed organization, the fact is that in these organizations the level of motivation is such that it can be done when necessary. Through their attitudes and policies, effective managers may create a reserve to be used in unusual conditions. Providing time off rather than "make-work" activities during periods of slack demand may influence employees to produce superhuman effort when needed.

Other firms are able to share capacity. For years Pan American leased aircraft to National Airlines during the winter season when National encountered peak demands for its Florida vacation flights and Pan American's European demand for travel between North America and Europe was reduced. Hospitals share specialized facilities that no single institution can use fully or even afford to operate at low levels of use.

If firms are able to take a sufficiently long view of their businesses, they build inventory in the form of excess capacity at times when it is less expensive to do so. A data-processing-service firm expanding its facilities or building anew might plan adequate conduits and wiring for a volume of activity several times that expected at the time of construction.

Finally, to the extent that servers can exercise judgment, they may limit operations performed during periods of peak demand, saving them for an off-peak period. A flight attendant may defer complicated passenger questions about flight connections until after the meal has been served.

In situations where supplies of services may be difficult to control, it may be possible to manage demand and its timing. The form of this management may vary. A utility institutes "peak load pricing," which penalizes those using power during times of typically high demand. A resort hotel may offer off-season packages at reduced rates; a hotel catering primarily to business travelers may do the same for weekends.

Customers asked to make reservations often benefit two ways. First, capacity is reserved for them, allowing for advance planning and lower costs (unless the capacity goes unused). Second, because of advance planning, the level of service provided often meets standards set for it, at least by the service firm. Nearly all reservation systems provide good examples of vehicles for inventorying demand and for managing capacity to meet that demand.[15]

DEVELOPMENT OF A "MEMBERSHIP" BASE

Some services rely on discrete transactions, such as the purchase of insurance for a specific trip; others involve the continuous delivery of service, as in the purchase of a life insurance policy. Some may be based on no formal relationship betweeen the customer and the firm providing the service. Yet others may be centered around a kind of "membership" relationship in the "club" operated by the service firm. Christopher Lovelock has described these kinds of relationships, shown in Table 3-2.

Subscription-oriented services provide the basis for developing a "membership" relationship between a company and its customers. On the one hand, the high costs of initiating individual sales are avoided; on the other hand, the information gained through the membership process can be used to improve the service in ways its

Table 3-2
Services with Membership Relationships with Customers

Service Delivery	Membership Relationship	No Formal Relationship
Continuous Delivery of Service	Insurance Telephone subscription College enrollment Banking American Automobile Association	Radio station Police protection Lighthouse Public highway
Discrete Transactions	Long distance calls from subscriber phone Theater series subscription Travel on commuter ticket	Car rental Mail service Toll highway Pay phone Movie theater Public transportation Restaurant

Source: Christopher H. Lovelock, "Classifying Services to Gain Strategic Marketing Insights," *Journal of Marketing* (Summer 1983) 13.

users consider significant. In any situation where continuous service as opposed to discrete transactions can be encouraged, costs can be reduced and demand known in advance. Once the American Automobile Association registers a member, it need only record the member's number each time the subscriber requests towing service. The same membership effect holds for members of "clubs" ranging from newspaper readers to credit card holders.[16]

CONTROL THROUGH "OWNERSHIP"

Ownership of assets often is less costly than rental or lease. While it may be beyond the means of new service ventures, it can provide an advantage for more well-established firms not only in terms of lower costs but in improved service as well.

When Emery Airfreight featured rapid delivery of small high-priority freight through the use of "blocked" or reserved space on airlines, avoiding the ownership of its own air fleet, Federal Express initiated a service featuring door-to-door control of shipments in equipment owned or leased by the company. A hard-hitting advertising campaign featured this difference. Whether Emery's service in fact suffered in comparison to that of Federal Express, customers began to perceive that it might suffer. Emery, previously regarded as the leader in its industry, was subsequently forced to lease or purchase aircraft of its own.

This type of control is not obtained without cost, usually reflected in the rate at which a firm is able to turn over its assets (its sales-to-assets ratio) and to change its asset base to reflect changing market needs. Consider the profit model in Table 3-1 for Allied Van Lines, a company that depends on a network to move household goods from point to point. Allied's relative investment in its network is much smaller than that for other transport carriers, including Federal Express, as we see in column 7 of Table 3-1. Allied relies on independently owned authorized agents for pick-up, storage, and delivery of shipments and on independent owner-operators of long-haul rigs for much of its long distance transportation.

SELECTIVE LEVERAGING OF SCARCE SKILLS

Many firms base their strategies on an ability to leverage the skills of their senior people with many more junior and less well-paid associates. A senior person selectively supervises at strategic points in a relationship, project, or process, or through the use of standardized procedures designed to produce a high-quality result with limited skill or judgment. The auditing divisions of large, public accounting firms rely on the development and maintenance of a pyramid of a small number of partners backed up by a larger number of associates and assistants. The fact that assistants perform most of the work and receive relatively low pay within the organization helps the entire firm to achieve an acceptable "multiple" of revenue-per-hour over the average hourly wages paid to its employees. High compensation is the outcome for a small number of partners; quality is almost as high as if the service were performed entirely by senior partners, but costs to the client are lower.

Of course, the pyramid has to be managed carefully. The numbers of people it can support at each level are determined by the volume of business it expects, the number of partners, associates, and assistants that it will require, and the rate at which personnel at each level are promoted, leave the firm, and are hired from outside.

The smaller the tip and the broader the base of the pyramid, the fewer the chances that people at lower levels can be promoted, the higher the likely exit rate at time of promotion (or lack of it), the higher the training costs for entry positions, and the lower the continuity of personnel in lower-level positions. All this is typical of large auditing organizations in public accounting firms.

Such firms rely on a high rate of turnover, particularly at the time of promotion from assistant to associate (usually after three or four years with the firm). They deliberately seek a high rate of turnover among the less desirable (or less highly motivated) assistants by offering positions requiring long hours, particularly during certain seasons of the year, and by paying low wages. To ease the training costs associated with high turnover, they rely on outside institutions (such as schools of business) to provide a portion of the training for incoming assistants. New recruits, understanding the nature of the "contract" with the firm, see such positions as offering good additional training, if not a life-long career. This symbiotic relationship is made possible by the firm's ability to leverage the value of its senior partners by using assistants whose skills are enhanced through standard auditing methods.

The assignment process, as Maister has pointed out, is critical to the success of this strategy.[17] Care must be taken to avoid excess use of less skilled people or mismatches between clients and servers that sometimes result from the server's lack of industriousness or inadequate functional knowledge of the industry.

SELECTIVE APPLICATION OF TECHNOLOGY

Greater opportunities for more significant gains from the future combination of people and technology exist in the service industries than in manufacturing. Relevant technologies start at levels as low as the use of the box bed in a motel to eliminate the back-breaking task of vacuuming under beds, and they rise to rather exotic levels such as the delivery of individualized analyses, news reports, and other types of information by means of extensive communications systems, large data bases, and sophisticated software programs for accessing the information. The delivery of cash on demand at any time of the day or night at locations remote from a banking institution or a teller, and diagnosing and even repairing automobile malfunctions are other examples.

In some industries, "high touch" (personal contact) will remain more important than high tech, particularly where there are high perceived risks associated with the service—financial, legal, medical, or social. Even here, opportunities for the introduction of technology abound. Service providers are learning to combine high tech with high touch by introducing the personal element into the service only at points judged critical to service quality and perceptions of that quality. It is quite likely that 90 percent of the most routine aspects of medical diagnosis will one day be performed by machines, with only the most critical 10 percent supplied by the doctor.

Levitt cites a number of examples of the selective application of what he terms both "hard" and "soft" technologies to the delivery of services.[18] In many cases, they reduce cost and also improve the perceived quality.

Electrocardiograms are among the hard technologies that can be operated by a technician with results interpreted by a doctor in less time and with more precision than if the doctor were to use a stethoscope. Airport X-ray surveillance equipment transforms the highly personal process of searching individuals into a relatively impersonal one performed by machine and operator.

Soft technologies such as well-organized job descriptions and assignments, prepackaged vacation services, and products like mutual funds designed to eliminate analysis and decision by the customer, may also achieve the same objectives.

SUBSTITUTION OF INFORMATION FOR ASSETS

Firms ostensibly competing in the same industry may have sharply different asset intensity, involving different investment patterns. Dow Jones must invest heavily in fixed assets to process and distribute worldwide each day its most well-known publication, *The Wall Street Journal*. But another firm in the information industry, CompuServe, makes available 1,400 different data bases that can be accessed only through the personal computers of its more than 200,000 (by recent count) subscribers. Much of the responsibility for investment in assets has shifted to the customer, leaving CompuServe with a "portfolio" heavily weighted toward investment in new forms of information rather than in fixed assets.

The Italian-based Benetton Group has pioneered a retailing approach throughout Europe that promises to influence a number of other retailers worldwide:[19] It substitutes information for assets. Because its first retail outlet offering knitted outerwear in colorful fashions was very small, the Benetton family developed an approach to retailing that makes effective use of small spaces. Unlike its more traditional competitors with stores of perhaps 4,000 square feet, the typical Benetton outlet is no more than 600 square feet. Little space is wasted for floor selling or for "back room" storage. An electronic communications system supported by a manufacturing process allows for dyeing to order and for rapid replenishment of items in greatest demand during a fashion season. The result is a higher rate of inventory turnover in the store and a level of sales-per-square-foot that is often several times that of Benetton's competitors. Benetton's assets support many more sales because it has injected both communications and production technology into its service.

MANAGING THE "MIX" OF PEOPLE AND EQUIPMENT

According to Dan Thomas, service industries can be compared on a scale in terms of the extent to which they are "people-based" or "equipment-based."[20] The financial implication is that the equipment-based service will be more asset-intensive, require more financial resources, and encounter greater difficulties in sustaining growth from the internal generation of cash.

Performances in 1983 for two companies listed in *Fortune*'s 100 largest diversified service companies, Hospital Corporation of America and ServiceMaster Industries, are shown in Table 3-1. The asset-intensity of the former compared with the latter is markedly different. HCA, a business employing large quantities of equipment and inventories in relation to people (in 1984, more than $61,000 in assets per employee), owns and operates hospitals in addition to supplying them. ServiceMaster provides much less exciting services to hospitals and other institutions: housekeeping and laundry, equipment maintenance, supplies ordering, and food preparation. ServiceMaster has a much lower ratio of equipment-to-people in the service packages it delivers.

Equipment-based firms like Hospital Corporation of America, usually employing higher levels of technology and often involved in higher tech operations, do not always outperform people-intensive services. Although HCA has consistently shown strong performance, ServiceMaster Industries in one recent decade was the most profitable of all 500 of the largest service firms.

MANAGING THE "SERVICE TRIANGLE"

A "service triangle" is composed of the service company, its employees (the servers), and its customers. The incidence of service businesses that have sunk due to the mismanagement of this triangle is as great as the alleged level of sinkings in another infamous triangle situated south of Bermuda.

The triangle, shown in Figure 3-4, consists of the players and their relationships.[21] The strongest relationship in some situations is between the server and the customer. When this relationship dominates the other two relations in the triangle (those between the company and the server on the one hand, and the company and the customer on the other), there is a strong possibility that the server may be able to retain the loyalty of the customer even if he or she leaves the employer. This knowledge may even tempt the server to leave. If not managed properly, the process is one in which the service company fosters its own future competition.

For years one of Merrill Lynch's great strengths has been its effective brokerage sales force. Each broker has been encouraged to build an individual business and has been compensated on the basis of a portion of the commissions earned on that business; for the most capable brokers, compensation can run into six figures.

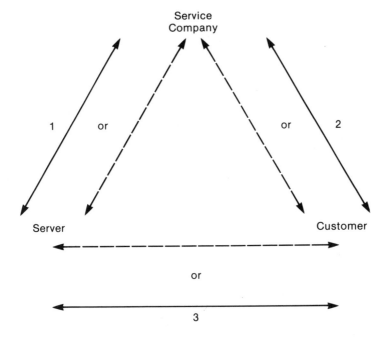

Relationship 1 is relatively strong,
while 2 and 3 are relatively weak.

Relationship 2 is relatively strong,
while 1 and 3 are relatively weak.

Relationship 3 is relatively strong,
while 1 and 2 are relatively weak.

◄- -► denotes a relatively weak relationship

◄——► denotes a relatively strong relationship

Configuration

Relationship 1 is relatively strong,
while 2 and 3 are relatively weak.

Relationship 2 is relatively strong,
while 1 and 3 are relatively weak.

Relationship 3 is relatively strong,
while 1 and 2 are relatively weak.

Likely Outcome

Servers are unwilling to move from
company to company.

Servers are unable to maintain
customer loyalty if they move from
company to company.

Highly mobile servers are able to
maintain customer loyalty as they
move from company to company.

Figure 3-4
The Service Triangle

At present, the company needs to broaden its product offerings to include other specialized service products such as insurance and real estate. It must therefore either reorient its brokers or establish direct relationships with customers. Either alternative is likely to alienate brokers, who frequently have much stronger relationships with their customers than does Merrill Lynch. As one veteran Merrill Lynch broker put it recently, "My customers are my blanket. I can just pick them up and walk away."[22]

The same dilemma confronts insurance companies that have traditionally worked through brokers but must now devise ways of marketing a much broader line of financial service products.[23]

Managers in firms finding themselves in this situation have sought ways to achieve better balance among relationships. Whenever possible, they make the firm and its collective capabilities more visible to the client. Alternatively, they increase compensation levels and incentives for capable employees to the point where individual practice is relatively less attractive.

FOCUS IN THE COMPETITIVE STRATEGY

Firms that focus their efforts on one type of customer or on doing one thing well for many types of customers often achieve low costs as well as high service standards. For more than twenty years, Eastern Airlines' Shuttle, connecting New York with Boston and Washington, has been one of the more successful airline operations. The service was designed for business travelers who make day trips and are uncertain about the exact time of their departure or return; it was intended to provide little more than guaranteed seats to its users. Anyone arriving at the gate before the time of departure was guaranteed a seat, even if Eastern had to call up an extra flight or "section" on short notice. This high-cost feature was at the very heart of Eastern's service concept. To offset the possible costs of this service and to allow for reduced fares, Eastern introduced a self-ticketing process in which both tickets filled out by the traveler and the fare were collected on board after take-off.

Although Eastern's clientele for the Shuttle often complained about its "cattle car" approach to air transport, people quietly valued its guaranteed service. In fact, through a succession of price increases after introducing the service, Eastern was not able to detect a price at which demand was severely curtailed.

A real test of the service occurred several years ago when New York Air, one of the first of the low-cost airlines, instituted parallel service offering more traditional reserved (as opposed to guaranteed) seats, preflight ticketing, and amenities en route. During the first year of its operation, Eastern believed the alternative service to have diverted no more than 8 percent of its business, even though tickets on New York Air were being sold at barely more than half the price of those on the beloved Shuttle.

Why are users loyal to the Shuttle, even though they complain? An important reason is that the guaranteed seat reduces anxiety. Another is that business travelers are creatures of habit. Those who travel once or more each week between cities served by the Shuttle know by habit exactly where to go and when. New York Air has had difficulty educating business travelers about the location of its terminals, even though it has been able to attract a number of less knowledgeable younger travelers for whom price is of great importance.

But there is one segment of the traveling public to which the Shuttle really represents superior service: the segment that does not enjoy interacting with airline ground employees. A business traveler catching the 7:00 A.M. Shuttle can arrive at the airport five minutes ahead of the flight, speak to no one before boarding, and be reasonably assured of an on-time arrival with a minimum of personal interaction. Through the years, the Shuttle has captured and held this customer.

Since 1907, United Parcel Service has offered dependable, low-cost delivery of packages over wide geographic areas. Its business customers, who provide nearly all of its revenue, understand this; its managers, who have resisted embellishing the service concept with additional objectives or "products," understand it; and its employees, who have to deliver the service, understand it.

One of the main reasons for UPS's strength is its emphasis on building route density (number of packages per stop and customers per route mile), standardizing the job of the route driver to allow for comparison and control, and designing its sorting facilities and transport equipment to handle packages of no more than 108 inches in combined length, width, and height and seventy pounds in weight. This single-minded approach to a service concept allows UPS to realize substantial profits while often charging its customers as little as half that of its competition. This, in turn, contributes to greater density and comparatively better service at lower rates. UPS now carries more than twice as many packages as its nearest rival, the U.S. Postal Service's parcel post. Recently UPS picked up, sorted, and delivered as many as 10 million packages a day with its fleet of 62,000 vehicles, including Boeing 727s.[24]

There is some question about how well a firm can deliver more than one level of service. The U.S. Postal Service recognized this several years ago when it abandoned its two-level surface and air mail service to provide just one letter delivery service at one rate. Many users had discovered that most of their mail was shipped by air whether they paid for it or not. But they became disgruntled on those occasions when they mailed a letter by surface and it was not shipped by air. When personal contact with the customer is important, attitudes and impressions conveyed by personnel delivering premium services one day and economy services the next may be counterproductive.

Once having achieved focus and the success that often accompanies it, why would a firm lose it? Sasser, Wyckoff, and Olsen have outlined the problem in their description of the life cycle of a multisite service firm, which encompasses the following stages: entrepreneurship, multisite rationalization (reproducing the concept), growth, and maturity.[25]

Managers of service firms that enter business maturity often have the demands of the investing public for continued growth ringing in their ears. They seek to find new concepts or new target customers. When the attempt is made in existing facilities or with the same management as for the focused business, focus, growth, and profits are often lost.[26]

Richard Normann, chairman of an international service firm, cites examples of this loss of focus: the acquisition of the luxury class Sofitel Hotels by French self-service, fast-food purveyor, Jacques Borel; efforts by Booz, Allen & Hamilton to add an executive search service to its management consulting service; and the attempted integration of its two basic services, cleaning and security, by the Danish firm, International Service System. Borel's fortunes plummeted and his businesses were acquired by a bank. Booz, Allen & Hamilton disbanded its executive search service. And International Service System "returned to a management system which, operationally, kept the two sides of the business more clearly apart."[27]

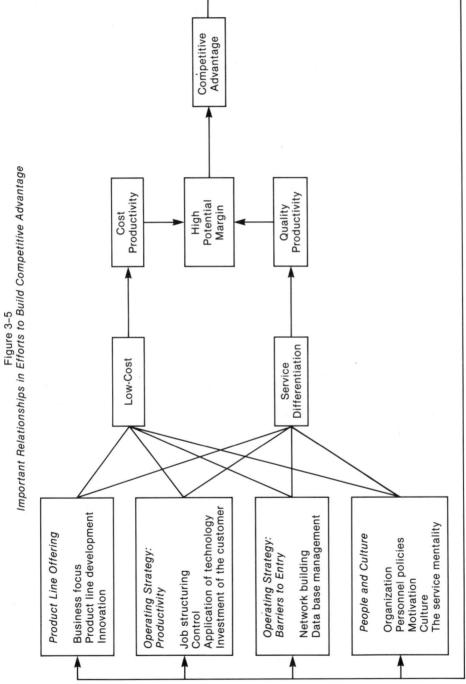

Figure 3-5
Important Relationships in Efforts to Build Competitive Advantage

In order to maintain focus under such circumstances, successful managers have: (1) resisted efforts to introduce new services through existing outlets or networks, or (2) created separate entrepreneurial entities, each with their own managements, to begin again the life cycle described above.

UPS's management has periodically analyzed the potential for expanding its promotional effort to emphasize door-to-door transportation for individuals as well as for commercial customers. Although it offers the door-to-door service on request, it has periodically rejected the notion of promoting it, because of the increased cost of serving uninformed individuals who frequently ship only one package as opposed to the more expert manufacturer or retailer from which several packages might be picked up or delivered in a single stop.

Positioning—developing low-cost, highly enhanced, or highly focused services—can be achieved through a carefully planned product line offering, increased productivity, the development of barriers to entry, and close attention to people and company culture. Low cost, high quality, and high degrees of focus of service all can lead to high productivity, if productivity is defined in terms of substantial operating margins. These operating margins provide the basis for competitive advantage, which in turn can provide opportunities for the further development of product line, operating strategy, and people. The dynamics of these interrelationships, as diagrammed in Figure 3-5, are elements of a strategy for maintaining competitive advantage in many service industries. They are the subject of the next four chapters: product line offering (Chapter 4), ways of achieving outstanding records of productivity (Chapter 5), barriers to competitive entry (Chapter 6), and the development of people and what will be called an effective service mentality (Chapter 7).

CHAPTER FOUR

The Service Concept
Product Line Development

Tom Staton,[1] an entrepreneur with a highly creative mind, decided to fashion a business strategy by offering services that other entrepreneurs might find unattractive: He wished to build a solid waste disposal service for commercial and industrial accounts in Denver, Colorado, that might make use of farmland on the outskirts of the city, in which he had bought a partnership. The idea was to dispose of inedible waste at a sanitary landfill to be developed on the farm and feed the edible waste to its pigs.

The solid waste disposal and pig farming businesses that Staton subsequently developed both thrived. The business really took off when Staton, who was able to place a significantly lower bid than his competition because of the fit with his existing businesses, won a major contract from the City of Denver for the demolition of several blocks of buildings as part of an urban renewal contract. Staton did not know much about demolition; he had to start a demolition business to satisfy the contract. But the contract called for the winner not only to demolish the buildings but also to haul the debris away and fill empty basements with dirt.

By now, Staton's product line was in place. His demolition company began its work. The debris was hauled to the farm and buried along with solid waste in sanitary landfill trenches from which dirt had been dug, and the debris brought from the city was replaced in the trucks by dirt to be hauled back to the demolition site for

75

basement fill material. Meanwhile, the farm's livestock continued to thrive on the edible garbage obtained from the solid waste disposal operation. Staton's companies served the city and his private customers well at very low prices. His profits were high.

Tom Staton is an example of a long line of service entrepreneurs that include early barbers, who developed a sideline that became dentistry as a way of filling their empty chairs. Leading service firms understand, as Tom Staton did, how to make a multiple-product strategy work for them. Not all elect one as intricate as his; some reject multiple businesses altogether in the interests of preserving product focus; and others center such strategies on elements other than products.

DEFINING THE BUSINESS

Effective product line strategies start with a clear business definition, one stated in terms of results produced for customers. The definition should not be so narrow that it exposes a company to surprises from firms in related industries. But a business definition should not be so broad that it leads to the development of new businesses outside a management's competence or ability to control.

Frederic V. Malik, hired as executive vice president of the Marriott Corporation in the mid-1970s, stated:

> In the early seventies, a serious effort was made to define what we were. What business were we in? The broadly defined answer was: leisure time. From there it was an easy jump from restaurants, contract feeding, and hotels to cruise ships and theme parks. We said: "Aren't theme parks just restaurants with entertainment? And aren't cruise ships floating hotels?"[2]

However well these new businesses fit with the broadly defined mission, they proved to defy existing abilities within the Marriott organization. Marriott's management therefore decided to reemphasize its strengths, opening more hotels, and helping a wider range of customers solve their institutional feeding problems.

Success has resulted from definitions broad enough to allow a firm to defend its core service business from surprise attacks from competition, but narrow enough to give the firm a reasonable chance of being a major player among competitors for the business. Thus, Dun & Bradstreet sold its highly profitable Corinthian

Broadcasting subsidiary because it did not fit with D&B's business definition of "providing information and services to business."[3] Some of the money from the sale was used to acquire Datastream, a British company supplying computerized information to business.

Defining the service carefully is a major problem among firms offering one or more financial services: banking, insurance, investment banking, real estate, and financial advisory programs. Today banks, insurance companies, real estate brokers, and investment banks all define their businesses as financial services. None of the leading institutions in these industries can take the chance of defining their businesses more narrowly, but they are all on a collision course. Further, they are being joined by firms whose bases of interest are as diverse as retailing and travel-related services.

Similar problems of business definition arise in companies in the communications and computing industries, whose paths are rapidly converging around a business definition of information. Publishers, broadcasters, data-base distributors, and others are joining them. Under these conditions, the matter of focus in the product strategy takes on increasing importance.

FOCUS

An examination of the business definitions and product portfolios of a number of the most successful service firms suggests that they seek to focus their efforts on customer segments, internal capability, geographic dominance, or some combination of these. While focus is not always reflected in their respective business definitions, it is implicit in what they do, the products they develop, and the businesses they acquire.

FOCUS ON CUSTOMER SEGMENTS

An outstanding performer among mass merchandisers, Wal-Mart Stores, Inc., has based its success on a strategy of serving customers in relatively small rural midwestern and southern communities with a selection of branded merchandise at low prices. The stores are anything but fancy, and management practices, many of them provided by the company's chairman and chief executive, Sam Walton, are often homespun; for example, handing out candy to customers in long lines at the checkout counters.[4]

This company's management knows what it can and will do best; just as important, it knows what it cannot and will not do.

American Express has sought to expand its range of services to its original base of customers: travelers, often on business, with relatively high incomes and with complex needs related to security and what has come to be known as funds transfer. The company has now assembled a variety of product capabilities: personal and property insurance, various investment vehicles, and increasing capability for using its former travel-oriented credit card as an instrument not only for obtaining cash but for carrying out other banking-related transactions. At the same time, the company has sought to make more effective use of its capabilities in the field of data processing, concentrating on services to customers that require massive data-processing activities in a timely and accurate manner.

Sears, Roebuck thought of itself until recently as a merchant to middle America. As a matter of fact, the company's customer base in 1981 was so large that it could hardly have been considered focused:[5] encompassing 25 million households that actively used Sears charge cards and 48 million, or 57 percent of all households, to which cards had been issued. For years the company centered its retailing efforts on a customer group characterized as suburban or rural, middle income, and interested in good value in moderately priced products purchased from a company that stands behind its products. The fact that Sears has attracted large numbers of customers with higher incomes and more highly urban orientations is testimony to the efficacy of Sears' strategy to implant itself firmly in the center of the demographic spectrum for many customer traits. And while many have argued that Sears' retail offerings have become somewhat confusing in recent years, studies have shown that the company retains a loyal customer base.

Around this base the company has begun to fashion a variety of offerings in financial services, including insurance (Allstate), real estate (Coldwell Banker), investments (Dean Witter), personal lending and flexible funds transfer (the Active Assets Account offered by Dean Witter). The financial services business is being conducted under the same roof as Sears' vast retailing activities, utilizing a common resource of distribution.

Firms focusing on a customer segment to which they may bring a variety of services rely primarily on a "halo" effect among their customers. The effect can cut both ways. Having enjoyed good service from Sears' retailing operations, a customer may be more willing to try the company's financial services. Indeed, that has been the company's experience in its initial efforts. On the other hand, poor service in one product can also influence a customer's willingness to try another. Companies pursuing a multiproduct strategy centered on a customer segment, must take great care to maintain control over the quality of the service each of their products provides or else maintain separate identity for their services in the customer's mind. In its relationship with Hyatt Legal Services, a low-cost purveyor of basic legal assistance, H & R Block has done both. It provides administrative and marketing services to Hyatt through a subsidiary, Block Management Company. But even though both services may share certain target markets and often are located in adjacent store-front offices, care is taken to maintain a separate identity for the two services.

This phenomenon is important in entire industries. It can be said that each of the prospective players in the financial service industry is betting its customer base against the others in the battle for position. And as the numbers in Figure 4-1 suggest, there is a great deal of overlap in the customers that such firms as Prudential, Citibank, Merrill Lynch, Aetna, American Express, and Sears call "their own." This suggests that the halo effect, in addition to the way in which each company implements its strategy, will be a major determinant of the outcome. The importance of this may be reduced only to the extent a customer is willing to use two or more companies' financial services, something which some of these firms may be trying to discourage and others encourage.

FOCUS ON INTERNAL CAPABILITY

On the surface, there is little rhyme or reason to the products offered by the Loews Corporation. Starting from a family hotel operation, the Tisch brothers, major owners of the company, acquired control of Loew's, a chain of motion picture theaters. They expanded their chain of Loew's hotels and they purchased a large insurance company, CNA Financial Corp. Along the way, they picked up Lorillard, a cigarette manufacturing company. In these assorted companies they have instituted strong controls, supplemented by financial reports and frequent personal contact, a particular capability of the company's management. In fact, in

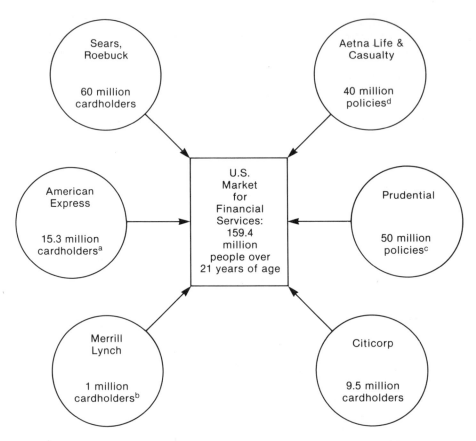

SOURCE: Published company documents and telephone conversations with company
    representatives.

[a]Worldwide: 20.7 million cardholders
[b]Corresponds to 1 million cash management accounts; Merrill Lynch also has 5
million accounts for its individual services.
[c]Number of policy certificates, i.e., people or items insured. In addition, Prudential-
Bache has about 1 million clients and 100,000 credit cardholders.
[d]Number of policy certificates, i.e., people or items insured.

Figure 4-1
Major Players in the U.S. Financial Services Industry, by Numbers of Credit
Cards or Accounts Outstanding, 1984

looking for acquisitions, they have selected businesses whose performance can be easily and quickly measured and supervised by a very small group of senior managers.[6]

American Airlines' most distinctive capability among its competitors may not be the ability to provide dependable air transport: Some among American Airlines managers are seeking ways to leverage the company's strong capability in developing and managing information and related communication systems. A recognized leader in this field among airlines since the development of its SABRE reservations systems, American is now developing additional products not aimed at travel. American Airlines Telemarketing Services (AATS) was recently formed to provide to other firms programs involving telephone selling, survey, or response services. In so doing, it is making off-peak use of American's vast phone reservations system which is structured to handle peak airline needs.

Other airlines have also sought to achieve better utilization of internal capabilities. United has begun to solicit business from the government as well as from other airlines to train pilots. USAir, Inc. has become so successful in disposing of excess equipment that it has gone into the aircraft brokerage business. Delta Airlines has begun servicing aircraft for other airlines. And Frontier Airlines has formed a new ground services company to serve both its own and other airlines' needs.[7]

Two consortia of airlines in Europe have been formed to take this concept one step further in aircraft maintenance. One of these, named KSSU (composed of KLM, SAS, Swissair, and UTA, a French charter operator), was formed in the 1970s to divide up the maintenance work for the combined fleets by type of aircraft or engine. Together they achieve maintenance costs comparable to much larger competitors, thus helping each to obtain "third-party" maintenance work from airlines not included in the consortium.

Federal Express has developed a line of products since the introduction of its small package delivery service in the 1970s. Its first new product was Courier Pak, an overnight delivery service for envelopes weighing up to two pounds. A more recent product called Overnight Letter provides the same service for lighter weight mail. All use the same operating network. Because Courier Paks and Overnight Letters can be stuffed into space not used by larger-sized packages, they can be carried with little additional expense by the company's fleet of aircraft.

Merrill Lynch has developed a major asset in its efforts to maintain its position as the largest investment brokerage company in the world. The Cash Management Account allows anyone with a Merrill Lynch account to have idle funds automatically "swept" into a high interest-bearing money fund. CMA was an immediate success and is a significant strength for the company.

Financial capability may influence a firm's development of its product line. Sears, Roebuck has about $3 billion outstanding at any one time in consumer loans on merchandise it sells. Its acquisition of Dean Witter, a securities broker with a capability for reinvesting money placed with it by its customers, provides a potential source of capital within the Sears organization.

This is what Tom Staton understood so well in putting together his "mini" service conglomerate in the Denver area. There was little focus in his customer base for the products his firm offered. His customers were industrial firms and the City of Denver. But each of the pairings of products benefited from an internal capability, whether it was real estate, a market for solid wastes, or an empty truck able to move debris in one direction and fill-dirt in the other.

GEOGRAPHIC FOCUS

Firms relying heavily on network-oriented economies associated with the "density" of their activity often seek to achieve significant market share in a geographic area. Thus, there has been a great deal of "trading" of slots at major airports as larger airlines seek to concentrate their efforts to build market share for traffic moving into and out of a small number of major geographic hubs.

Xerox and IBM are dependent on the quality of their service networks to maintain competitive advantage. For them, high market share in a particular geographic area means higher customer density and an increased ability to respond rapidly to requests for service at lower costs than competitors holding lower market shares. Competitors have been able to break this kind of hammerlock only by concentrating sales efforts on certain geographic markets and avoiding others, often putting in place a much larger service organization than a market might warrant. Their hope is to gain market share and customer geographic density to justify the investment.

Advertising, too, creates a kind of "network effect." Retailers of fast food cluster their outlets in targeted markets to defray important advertising expenses. Kroger, now the largest grocery retailer in the United States, closed more than 1,200 supermarkets in recent years in an effort to concentrate its business in an area within a box having corners at Indianapolis, Memphis, Chattanooga, and Columbus, Ohio. It can thereby realize economies not only in its advertising but in other activities benefiting from "scale of density," such as physical distribution. It now ranks first or second in eleven of its thirteen major food marketing territories, with a market share of about 50 percent in Ohio.[8]

ILLUSORY FOCUS

The Ryder System's truck leasing and rental division offers a complete service of long-term or short-term rental or lease with maintenance, if desired by the customer.[9] Ryder has relied on its ability to purchase and service trucks efficiently to provide the common element of its portfolio of services. But a closer look suggests that Ryder's customers are composed of either local or nationally oriented lessors, who use the trucks over vastly different geographic areas with attendant variations in needs for service. Those who rent vehicles for shorter periods of time range from individuals moving their household goods in one-way transportation over long distances to local firms seeking to meet short-term needs within a particular geographic area.

Marketing to individuals primarily through the Yellow Pages is greatly different from attempting to sell a corporation's top management on the financial advantages of a long-term truck lease. Servicing vehicles in a small number of locally oriented markets, as is typical in the local lease and rental business in which vehicles are based in one place, is greatly different from providing a service network for customers whose leased or rented vehicles roam the entire nation.

The system of controls that Ryder devised for maintenance and the way it organized its marketing effort forced the company to recognize that it was actually operating several businesses that had the truck in common only superficially.

At Federal Express, "communications"-oriented products like Courier Pak, Overnight Letter, and more recently Zap Mail, utilizing long-distance electronic transmission, have been good ways to complement its basic overnight package delivery service.[10] How-

ever, customers for the basic package delivery service offered by
Federal are typically manufacturing firms, often turning out items
of high value or of a critical nature. Such customers are willing to
pay for premium delivery service. The decision to use a particular
carrier may be made by a traffic manager or a shipping clerk, often
with an office located near the shipping dock. Consider, then, the
problems of superimposing on this business Courier Pak, overnight shipment of up to two pounds, usually documents. Courier
Pak users are primarily "paper factories" such as professional service firms. The decision to ship is made by executives or their
secretaries, whose offices rarely include a shipping dock.

Federal Express's managers finally recognized that they had
two different businesses requiring separate and different approaches to sales and advertising. They also needed additional
ground operations for pick-ups and deliveries of Courier Paks at
locations different from those for packages. The business then began to develop rapidly with high, incremental operating margins.

Leasing trucks was as illusory a focus for the Ryder System as
was package delivery for Federal Express.

MANAGING NEW PRODUCT DEVELOPMENT

The development of the product line, involving the design and
introduction of new service offerings, has been cited as one of the
more difficult challenges of managers in the service sector. According to those who have provided consulting services both to
manufacturing and service firms:

> New product development is inherently more difficult, messier, and
> less successful in the service sector. In industry, R & D labs can usually
> come up with new designs that incorporate certain predictable func-
> tions and characteristics. On the other hand, when a service firm cor-
> rectly, if subjectively, perceives a need, it cannot have the same
> confidence in its ability to deliver all the ingredients that comprise
> successful new service products. As a result, service organizations are
> more likely to be conservative about innovations. They focus most of
> their attention on geographical extensions of their service, or on minor
> modifications to the primary service package. True inventiveness is
> rare . . . innovation in the service sector is frequently the result of trial
> and error. . . . Original or imitative ideas exist in abundance. Yet, new
> ideas often ignore the deep and subtle linkages among the variables in
> the service package. Between imagination and execution lies a dark
> gulf that has swallowed up many a bright new product.[11]

Even with inherent difficulties involved, every service industry has companies and managers noted for their ability to foster new product development or the design and implementing of new internal processes. In banking, Citicorp is often mentioned among larger banks, Banc One among regional banks, and VISA among those providing cash transfer service systems. In financial services, Merrill Lynch, in spite of its size, is often the first to churn out novel products that are imitated by others. Dun & Bradstreet relies on new product development for a significant share of its revenue. In communications, Dow Jones and Gannett are frequently mentioned; in food and lodging, McDonald's and Marriott.

How do managements of these companies succeed in maintaining the spirit of entrepreneurship? First, they establish a culture for new product development, then they organize to foster it. Ideas may be generated in large numbers, but they must also be tested carefully with extensive monitoring, even of nonfinancial measures. And successful companies reward risk-takers.

ESTABLISHING A CULTURE

A culture supports entrepreneurship through a combination of legends, heroes, and actions.

While favorite stories at Citicorp are told about people who took risks and failed, more often the risk-taker succeeded. Establishing this kind of culture occurs at the top. As Walter Wriston, recently retired chairman of Citicorp said, "I'm a bureaucrat now, but once I was a dealmaker, and that was the most fun." His successor is John Reed, whose major accomplishment was to doggedly lead the eventually successful individual banking business at Citicorp through years of huge losses.[12]

When John G. McCoy assumed the presidency of City National Bank, the predecessor of Banc One, from his father in 1958, he took two actions very important to the entrepreneurial spirit of the bank. First, he created a research and development effort:

> I asked the board of directors—my father's friends, not mine—to approve setting aside 3% of earnings annually for research and they said, "We're a bank. Why do we need research?" And I said, "I don't know. That's what I want to find out." The board approved the request—"We weren't making $1 million a year, so $30,000 wasn't much"—and I began to explain how technology might help [the bank] do its job more efficiently.[13]

Second, McCoy followed the advice of an associate and hired a young radio "ad man," John Fisher, as head of a newly created advertising department. He commissioned Fisher to "find out what the customer wants," and forbade him to learn how to open an account or make a loan.[14] A stream of firsts followed. Banc One was the first smaller bank to offer a bank card, to develop computer processing capability, to combat credit fraud with color photos on its cards, to introduce a debit card, and to conduct experiments with retailers to replace checks with electronic transfers.

All this eventually led Banc One to preeminence in card processing and to the establishment of a Financial Card Services business that has become the largest in the country. When its first and largest customer, Merrill Lynch's Cash Management Account and associated VISA card, decided recently to process its own transactions, Banc One was large enough to concentrate its efforts on some 200 other customers that were offering CMA-type accounts. By then, for example, it had put in place an agreement with Comp-U-Card International, Inc. to issue interest-generating VISA credit cards to 250,000 of Comp-U-Card's members, who buy merchandise by telephone or home computer.[15]

Banc One is now among the leaders in developing home banking capabilities by bringing together various technologies. To head up its Channel 2000 projects, the bank assigned a recent business school graduate, who remarked, "The great thing about this place is that they give you an idea and let you run with it."[16] All this from a Columbus, Ohio, bank far from the so-called money centers but operating in a culture fostered by its former president.

The head of VISA International has similarly emphasized that his one guiding principle for the provider of cash transfer services for its banks and other customers is that "anything that might strangle innovation is bad."[17]

Finally, the right to voice contrary opinions is fostered, honored, and protected in the successful entrepreneurial culture. There is a strong ethic that supports those who speak their minds in these organizations, unlike some of their competitors who have installed electronic polling devices among senior executives to allow them to voice their views anonymously.

ORGANIZING TO FOSTER NEW PRODUCT DEVELOPMENT

To foster the drama of new product development, a cast of characters is required.[18] The "senior sponsor" is someone who has earlier been given an opportunity to try, and who possesses the influence and authority to insure that others be given the same opportunity.[19]

The second role is played by the "product champion," someone or some group that can provide both continuity and enthusiasm to a project. Given the tremendous frustrations and disappointments experienced in even successful product development, a champion is needed to see a project through to its conclusion.

Because most entrepreneurial efforts are multifunctional, they require inputs from an "integrator," someone with a multifunctional background and with the sensitivity to encourage coordinated effort through persuasive abilities rather than from a position of authority.

The final actor is the "referee," a counterbalance in the entrepreneurial process. The referee's task is to develop and gain acceptance of the rules by which performance will be evaluated. Once in force, such rules must then be administered by the referee in approving new projects, killing existing ones, or both.

The cast is often organized around successful project, product, or development managers, or the groups that have come to be called new venture teams. By designating a "champion" as manager of the project, product, or development, many firms obtain the concentrated effort and enthusiasm they need to sustain a new idea. For more substantial, longer-term projects, a venture team comprising several managers with requisite skills may be needed, and they often are allowed to manage a successfully developed new business during its early years.

Firms most successful in sustaining strong new product development effort will employ several such organizational forms; they may also encourage competition among various "product champions" in the development of a new idea. Instead of assigning one task force to determine how best to develop an insurance business, Citicorp formed three. This requires a depth of management but it also is a vehicle for building management depth.[20]

TESTING IDEAS IN THE MARKETPLACE

Firms successful in developing new ideas for products or businesses have developed means for testing them carefully. For most service businesses this means a major reliance on market testing as opposed to concept or product testing.

Market testing is the most feasible way of determining whether the public will use a largely intangible service. Since there is no product to subject to a series of tests, a service concept is often difficult to describe to a prospective customer. It may elicit misleading responses when "tested" through pictures and words.

Managers must weigh the advantages of gaining added information on market acceptance through market testing against the potential for disclosure of new concepts to potential competitors. Nonetheless, for complex new services requiring significant commitment of capital, a long period of testing may be desirable. During this time, the emphasis is on maintaining flexibility, hedging risk by avoiding commitment to long-term investment or to high fixed costs, and, above all, experimenting.

The home banking system that Citicorp recently introduced was the product of four years of market testing in Washington, D.C., and Denver. Marriott's new low-overhead, moderately-priced chain of as many as 300 Courtyard hotels is being developed after the recent successful test operation of three for more than a year in Atlanta. The company is now planning tests of all-suite luxury hotels, time-sharing condominiums, and "lifecare" communities for the over-65 market.[21] McDonald's recently has been testing two McSnack stand-up restaurants and one McStop interstate highway complex.

MONITORING RESULTS

Successfully controlled new product or business development prominently involves the referee, who in conjunction with the product champion establishes guidelines for success, specific benchmarks, and a set of ground rules "for determining successes and failures."

It can be difficult for service businesses to determine product profit or loss because of the high incidence of costs that are common to two or more products. Guidelines or benchmarks must therefore be stated in terms of volume of sales, transactions, or service delivered against budgets for costs attributable to the service in question. Customer reactions may be tracked and factored into such measurements.

Predetermined ground rules are the best antidote to "benchmark creep," the sliding of goals or deadlines for their achievement. By agreeing in advance that some number of consecutive failures to achieve the incremental progress established for successive benchmarks means project termination, several successful service firms have managed the most difficult task of selectively encouraging good ideas. They have also been able to kill poor ones with little argument or discouragement to the entrepreneurial spirit they have tried to foster.

REWARDING RISK-TAKERS

Edwin P. Hoffman bought a Lebanese bank for his employer, Citibank, just before civil war broke out in Lebanon. Until then, his pet project of building an overseas data-processing business for the bank had been a failure. But while experiencing these setbacks, he was building the company's institutional business in the Middle East and Africa. His reward was appointment as executive vice president in charge of Citibank's Individual Bank branch network in the United States outside New York City.[22]

Dow Jones' most ambitious new ventures in the field of electronic publishing have been led by William Dunn, building on the long-established news-ticker known as the Dow Jones News Service. One of his successes has been Dow Jones News/Retrieval, a service that delivers stock quotes and news to clients by computer. He does not succeed every time:

> In 1981 he started a service called Dow Alert that beamed the news on the broad tape over an FM frequency. Subscribers got a black box that they could program to track stories about specific companies or other subjects. The box would blare out the relevant stories as they were broadcast and record them for playback later. Dow Alert died. . . . "It really wasn't a radio, and it really wasn't a tape recorder," says Dunn. "It was like an aardvark. People didn't understand what it was." Undaunted, Dunn replaced Dow Alert with something called Dow Phone. As the name suggests, Dow Phone lets users call a phone number and listen to the latest word on whatever it is they follow.[23]

In 1984 William Dunn was promoted to executive vice president and was thought to be under consideration as one of the three or four individuals to succeed Dow Jones' chairman.

Innovative organizations have found ways of rewarding those who have taken good risks, even when they have not been consistently successful. At the same time, they have tried to develop better methods of measuring risk and of communicating such methods to individual managers who are given authority to act as entrepreneurs on behalf of their employers.

The results achieved in developing new products and businesses speak for themselves. Merrill Lynch has pioneered the Cash Management Account, which has served as a model for emulators while enabling Merrill Lynch to extend its services to include real estate, insurance, relocation, and even data communications services. Time Inc. set the pace in pay television with its Home Box Office and related businesses. Gannett has developed and introduced from scratch a national newspaper featuring innovations in design and distribution. MCI has risen from nowhere to challenge AT&T and others with its long-distance communications and related services. In a cyclical industry not characterized by rapid growth, Marriott's earnings increased at the compounded annual rate of 24 percent during the past five-year period. And although McDonald's is the largest food service operation in the world, it has steadily increased its share of market in recent years.

And, one of the larger public accounting firms, Arthur Young, pioneered perhaps the epitome of all innovative services, the innovation audit. Its purpose is to assess "whether a corporate structure allows new ideas to flourish."[24]

Once new services are formulated, tested, and introduced, their successful implementation requires long-term follow-through and a style of management that places emphasis on matters of productivity, the maintenance of competitive advantage through the development of barriers to entry, and people. They are the centers of our attention in the next three chapters.

CHAPTER FIVE

Operating Strategy
Productivity

There is an ongoing debate about the relative levels and rate of growth in productivity in the service sector. (See Appendix C.) Nevertheless, it is generally agreed that communications have led all sectors of the services economy in productivity improvement in recent years and that some firms—industrial and service—have had outstanding increases in productivity. From these firms important lessons are to be learned, particularly in the areas of job restructuring, control programs, the application of technology, and the involvement of the customer in the service delivery process.

JOB RESTRUCTURING

Job restructuring has been a hot topic in the industrial world. Managements have sought and received greater flexibility in the structuring of jobs when negotiating labor-management agreements. It has been a factor in improved productivity in services as well. But it has taken on a somewhat different character in jobs involving low customer contact.

LOW CONTACT JOBS

In low contact jobs, often in the "back offices" of data-handling operations, restaurant commissaries, and equipment repair facilities, a wide variety of job restructuring efforts resembling those

91

implemented in industry have been attempted, many with great success.

Some firms have moved beyond this stage. At Kemper Insurance, much of the gain from improved productivity of clerical staff has already been realized. Kemper is concentrating its efforts on "higher salaried managers and professionals by reorganizing the way they deliver insurance services. For example, one Kemper division found that its underwriters were doing jobs that could be reassigned to clerical workers, including filing, photocopying, and analyzing applications for assigned-risk pools for workers' compensation."[1]

Service firms, like industrial manufacturing companies, are discovering the difference between focus in a service operation and breaking down jobs into their simplest components. Services that focus on customer, product, or geographic area and yet structure jobs to reflect higher education levels of their servers are achieving considerable success. Consider the server in the back office of a major bank:

> At Continental Illinois National Bank & Trust Co. of Chicago, where there are no clerical unions, Christine Szcesniak worked for 17 years on a check-processing line, performing one function over and over. Now she works at a computer terminal in a "modular" arrangement and performs nearly all the tasks necessary to handle checks sent in by companies that buy goods and services from some 3,000 corporate clients by Continental. "I think it's exciting and different," Szcesniak says. "It's cut down on error ratio, and that's very important for me."
>
> Szcesniak now processes checks that arrive in the mail, deposits them in customers' accounts by computer, telephones customers with up-to-date information on their accounts, and mails the data to them. Under the automated system, each employee processes an average of 50 checks per hour, a 40% increase in productivity over the old approach. "I like it," Szcesniak says, "because you see the package from beginning to end. It's better to be part of the whole thing. Everyone should have change in their life."[2]

HIGH CONTACT JOBS

The challenge of job restructuring is somewhat different in jobs involving high customer contact where appearances may play as important a role as actual results.

For years Delta Airlines maintained greater flexibility in job assignments than any airline in the United States, with a long history of good labor relations. One of the major factors in Delta's flexibility is that employees are not restricted to a single job by union rules but rather are trained and willing to take on multiple jobs, an important contribution to profitability.

The formula has proven so attractive that, with the deregulation of the airline passenger industry in the United States, other airlines, notably the fastest growing, People Express, have been founded on a nonunion philosophy. People's pilots fly for less than half the salaries of their counterparts at other longer-established major airlines, even Delta. But People is their company: All employees own its stock. And once they have flown the 100 hours maximum per month permitted by safety rules, they are prepared to perform jobs that range from baggage handling to schedule planning. The passenger is even more likely to see one employee performing several jobs at People than at Delta. As a result, employee productivity at People Express has been more than twice that of the airline industry average, allowing the airline to charge fares from 45 to 75 percent lower than its competitors, get higher utilization out of its aircraft, and still realize the second highest margins on revenue of all airlines in one recent year.[3]

The problem is that the customer expects to see this at People Express, where low fares and no-frills service are celebrated publicly and the customer is likely to be younger than the employee. They do not expect to see it at a well-established airline that has traditionally emphasized premium transportation for customers who are, more often than not, older than its employees and more demanding.

An operating strategy and a service delivery system may both have to be designed to mask restructuring in jobs that might not otherwise meet customer expectations. At Benihana of Tokyo restaurants, the chef prepares food at a hibachi in front of the guests, combining the jobs of waiter and chef. At the conclusion of the meal, the chef punctuates his performance (and indirectly signals guests that it is time to leave) by cleaning the hibachi. Given the nature of a service concept that combines quality food and entertainment at reasonable prices as well as the exotic format of a Japanese restaurant, customers of Benihana readily accept a highly economic combination of jobs that is carried out in their full view.

CONTROL PROGRAMS

Success in services is linked closely to effective controls on quality, costs, assets, and labor.

QUALITY CONTROL

In contrast to the emphasis on cost control in large manufacturing firms, leading service enterprises have placed much greater emphasis on the control of quality. There are several possible reasons.

First, those who have held senior management positions in both service and manufacturing firms agree that the control of quality is much more difficult in the former. James L. Schorr, then executive vice president-marketing for Holiday Inns, Inc., but with previous experience at Procter & Gamble, states:

> I suppose a major difference between product marketing is that we can't control the quality of our product as well as a P&G control engineer on a production line can control the quality of his product. When you buy a box of Tide, you can reasonably be 99 and 44/100% sure that this stuff will work to get your clothes clean. When you buy a Holiday Inn room, you're sure at some lesser percentage that it will work to give you a good night's sleep without any hassle, or people banging on the walls and all the bad things that can happen to you in a hotel.[4]

These sentiments are echoed by Robert L. Catlin, then senior vice president-management supervisor at N. W. Ayer ABH International, a major advertising agency responsible for the AT&T account, but with previous experience at Vick Chemical Co.:

> In a service business, you find that you're dealing with something that is primarily delivered by people—to people. Your people are as much of your product in the consumer's mind as any other attribute of that service. People's performance day in and day out fluctuates up and down. Therefore, the level of consistency that you can count on and try to communicate to the consumer is not a certain thing.[5]

This is particularly true, of course, for firms whose employees maintain close contact with the customer in the delivery of the services.

Second, consistently high quality in a service is often linked directly to high productivity. Services of uneven quality may even be more costly to the company.

> When William J. Latzko came to New York's Irving Trust Co. in 1970 as its first quality-control officer, he found the bank's management disturbed because the machines were rejecting so many checks—

though nobody knew what the percentage was. Using standard statistical methods of quality control, Latzko found out how many checks were being rejected (it was 7 1/2 %) and why. It turned out that certain check manufacturers were doing a poor job of printing magnetic characters and some of the encoding machines were unreliable. Once these and other problems had been corrected, the rejection rate dropped to less than 2%.[6]

Third, many service firms have had limited success in costing their services in order to institute cost control programs. Indeed, John Dearden has raised serious questions for service firms about the validity of traditional approaches to cost accounting for other than the simplest measurements against budgeted costs.[7]

Finally, many firms in the service industries, including banks, financial services, utilities, and transportation firms, structure costs to be shared jointly by services and departments. Once the activity and staffing levels are set for a given period, most costs in these service operations are fixed. However, unit costs can be reduced below plan by activity, capacity utilization, and productivity that are higher than expected. In the long run the best way is to deliver service of consistent quality.

Measurements must be taken to establish standards of quality as well as performance against those standards. Approaches to jobs producing high-quality results must be clearly described, and such information must be communicated through training programs. And follow-up assistance to servers not measuring up to expectations must be performed.

Setting quality standards requires the careful measurement of both service and customer perceptions of quality. For some years American Airlines has measured on several dimensions the actual service levels delivered to its customers and those of its competitors. Comparing these results with reactions about the acceptability of the services experienced by these same customers provides the basis for establishing service standards. Recent standards required that 85 percent of passengers should have to wait in line to buy tickets no more than five minutes, reservation phones had to be answered within twenty seconds, airplane doors had to be opened no more than seventy seconds after the plane pulled up to the gate, and 85 percent of flights were to land within fifteen minutes of scheduled arrival time. This information is then used to determine staffing levels at various operating stations, for procedures, and for managers' pay and promotion.[8]

American Express has tried to improve the quality of its customer service with no increase in personnel while handling credit card requests and losses.[9] American Express's credit cardholders are interested in timeliness, accuracy, and company responsiveness. The company shares these interests, because it determined several years ago that it loses about $2.70 in charge volume for each day its card is unavailable for use. It also risks encouraging a customer to use a competitor's card.

Accordingly, the company formed employee task forces to examine various opportunities for improved performance by breaking down all service operations into their basic elements, measuring each, and then devising ways to improve them. One task force discovered that it took thirty-five days to process an application for a credit card. A survey suggested that applicants became impatient after three weeks, so that interval provided a new standard of quality. The cause of poor quality was a complex flow of documents and information between different departments. Because managers of the involved departments were included on the task force, one regional director for customer service remarked that "the system forces the walls between departments to come down." The standard for quality is now being met. A similar approach to reports of lost credit cards has reduced processing time from two or more weeks to as little as two days.

Quality control in operations not involving direct customer contact may resemble that in a manufacturing operation. It is aimed at reducing the error rate, nearly always with accompanying increases in productivity. But the nature of the quality control problem is even more complex when customer contact is involved, particularly when some of the most poorly paid employees are the contacts. Former president of Restaurant Operations at Marriott Corporation, G. Michael Hostage, speaks to this point:

> "The Marriott Bellman" booklet is designed to convince our uniformed doormen that they represent an all-important first and last impression for many of our guests, that they must stand with dignity and good posture, and that they must not lean against the wall or put up their feet when sitting. . . . Bellmen are often looked at subconsciously by guests as being "Mr. Marriott himself," because many

times a guest will speak to and deal with the bellman more often during a visit than with any other employees of the hotel. . . . They are coached to smile often and do all they can to make the guest feel *welcome* and *special.*[10]

Marriott's management thus establishes standards for every aspect of this and other jobs, communicates them through a series of booklets and detailed training, and follows up with a "flying squad" of inspectors. Through personal development, profit sharing, and stock ownership programs, it gives its first-line employees a reason to take an interest in the quality of service delivered.

COST CONTROL

Important as quality control is to the successful service operation, cost control has taken on increasing significance in certain service industries, particularly those that no longer enjoy the margin protection provided by past practices.

Bankers are now faced with both greater competition for money and the relaxation of restrictions on the interest rates that banks can pay depositors. Their costs of money, at one time fixed comfortably below the rates at which it could be loaned, have skyrocketed. Banks that traditionally offered a myriad of interrelated services, many at costs bearing no relation to the amounts charged customers, have thus been forced to take a new look at their costs on a product-by-product basis.

In health care, the U.S. government has instituted a new fixed-fee approach to contain rapidly escalating costs of its Medicare program. Hospitals are being reimbursed a fixed amount for Medicare charges for each of some 468 different diagnoses, forcing them to track costs patient by patient, doctor by doctor, and ailment by ailment. As John P. McDaniel, president of the Washington Hospital Center in Washington, D.C., said: "Before, what was driving the system was quality; in effect, money was no object. Now we're told the number one priority is cost-effective health care."[11]

John Dearden has argued persuasively that much of cost accounting for manufacturing has little relevance for service firms. He points out, "Many service organizations have little or no direct material and direct labor and limited amounts of variable overhead" that can be attributed to a business, a service product, or an operation.[12] Few service firms produce for inventory. The single most important use of cost accounting, inventory costing for tax and profit reporting purposes, is hence irrelevant.

Many service firms have no basis for assessing the profitability of anything other than the entire business, or they rely primarily on the budgeting process and the control of expenses against budget as their major form of cost control.

Attempts to assign all costs, including those unique to a given service and those costs incurred jointly by all services, have often produced startling results. One survey of fifteen advertising agencies that assigned all costs concluded that "of the 566 clients they served, 209 were unprofitable."[13] But such efforts, as Dearden has argued, may produce misleading conclusions.

Banks and investment banking firms with highly complex product lines have sought instead to identify only revenues and costs unique to a given product: those that would not be received or incurred, respectively, if the product were not offered. This provides a basis for ranking products by profitability. It may suggest products that can be dropped to achieve the greatest positive impact on both profitability and productivity with little impact on revenues or customer service.

Services in which a product is produced as part of the service do make use of standard costing techniques. In newer systems, unit sales are recorded electronically along with sales information at the cash register. For example, the operating management of a chain of fast-food restaurants can relate hamburger purchase costs to the number of hamburgers actually sold. Stores with pilferage or waste can be tracked and corrected. In other cases, controllable costs can be compared from one unit to another having comparable volume of activity. Such is the case in a national public warehousing organization operating many warehouses where part-time labor can be managed to meet day-to-day fluctuations in material-handling activity.

Many leading service executives in industries where few costs vary directly with volume have concluded that the best form of cost control is to expand sales using the existing service delivery system. Once the decision has been made to fly a plane on an airline's schedule (a decision made only two to four times a year), the costs to an airline of an additional passenger may be no more than 5 percent of revenue. Once the decision is made to operate an airline with a certain level of equipment and crew, the cost to schedule an additional flight may be no more than 30 percent of the revenue associated with a normal load. Under these conditions, one more passenger can significantly affect profitability (and costs as a proportion of revenue).

ASSET CONTROL

The best-run service managements devote a great deal of attention to the sizing of their operations and the general control of assets. Asset control often involves determining what capacity to offer customers (sizing the facility). It may be implemented through infrequent decisions. It is particularly difficult for fixed facilities. A restaurateur may get only one crack at it; and, for a new restaurant, the decision has to be made before the start of business. An airline may "size" its schedule, and thus its *active* fleet of aircraft several times a year, but its management has far fewer opportunities to vary the actual size of the fleet upward or downward.

Sizing is a question constantly confronting service firms having high fixed costs and severe peaks and valleys in the demand for their services. The most successful of those starting up often are those that are able to avoid fixed investment. They thus maintain asset flexibility in exchange for higher initial costs (largely those varying with the volume of business).

Firms unable to avoid substantial fixed investments, and having exhausted all management approaches to reducing peak demand, have to decide the proportion of peak demand they can afford to serve with emergency high-cost measures or not at all. The question constantly faces utility company managers. While they cannot fail to meet peak demand, they may have alternatives for doing it. The most effective has been the creation of power grids, bringing together cooperating power companies to aggregate greater quantities of demand and supply and thus dampen the extreme demands on the grid as a whole. This has allowed each member to meet a lower percentage of its own peak demand with its own assets, thus improving its rate of asset utilization.

Other firms, such as household goods movers, have greater discretion about what proportion of the particularly severe school-vacation moving business peak to serve. Given the steepness and infrequency of the peak and the ready availability of owner-operators who may be willing to contract to take on additional loads during peak times, this type of service firm may choose to meet only its base needs with its own trucks and with employees that can be kept busy on a year-round basis.

LABOR CONTROL

Labor makes up half or more of the costs of all professional service firms, educational institutions, hospitals, most financial institutions, and many transportation and other service firms. The way in which labor is utilized can mean the difference between success and failure.

A basic issue in the control of labor costs is the extent to which an effort should be made to adjust staffing levels to fluctuations in the amount of demand for service: whether demand should be "chased" or whether level staffing should be maintained. Many of the questions associated with this issue are raised by Earl Sasser in describing an example involving two departments in the headquarters of a national investment brokerage house.[14] Wide swings in volume take place on an unpredictable basis in the brokerage business, sometimes involving trading volumes that double or triple from one day or week to the next and random external events.

In Sasser's example the cashiering department responsible for handling and accounting for stock certificates and other documents associated with transactions is managed on a chase-demand philosophy. Skill requirements are relatively low, training can be accomplished rapidly, and labor turnover is over 100 percent per year. These factors encourage staffing policies that reflect the changing volume of business, and they permit forecasting and budgeting of activity levels on short notice.

By contrast, the information processing department in the same firm employs more highly skilled people trained to work with a large bank of data-processing equipment under conditions in which accuracy and quality of effort are very important. The firm has consciously invested in staffing and equipment capacity beyond the maximum demand encountered during recent peaks, and it maintains capacity at that level. The savings in training and error reduction more than offset the costs of maintaining unneeded capacity. And the very nature of the commitment requires long-range forecasting and budgeting.

Conditions under which the chase-demand and level-capacity strategies make the most sense for this firm are shown in Table 5-1.

Table 5-1
Comparison of Chase-Demand and Level-Capacity Strategies
for the XYZ Brokerage Firm

	Chase Demand	*Level Capacity*
Labor-skill level required	Low	High
Job discretion	Low	High
Compensation rate	Low	High
Working conditions	Sweatshop	Pleasant
Training required per employee	Low	High
Labor turnover	High	Low
Hire-fire costs	High	Low
Error rate	High	Low
Amount of supervision required	High	Low
Type of budgeting and forecasting required	Short run	Long run

Source: W. Earl Sasser, Jr., "Match Supply and Demand in Service Industries," *Harvard Business Review* (November-December, 1976): 135.

Although they may be representative of other firms' experiences as well, it is important to avoid creating a situation in which the very policy influences the profile and behavior of the labor force. To assume that high turnover and low training costs are appropriate for a particular strategy may encourage such a high level of turnover that assumed cost relationships do not hold, thus requiring an adjustment in the strategy itself.

Many efforts to enhance repetitive, low-skill jobs have resulted in reduced training costs and increased productivity levels that more than outweigh costs of maintaining excess capacity. More often, a base level of skilled labor capable of performing a number of tasks provides an assured capability for handling minimum levels of demand that can be supplemented with short-term or part-time labor needed to meet peak demands.

Union work rules restricting assignments have frequently made it difficult to achieve high labor utilization rates without resorting to chase-demand strategies of the sort described. But service firms committed to long-term relationships between employers and employees have been among the first to win less restrictive work rules allowing employees to be trained for several jobs and shifted from one to another, depending on peaks and valleys in demand for each element of the firms' services. A greater investment in people and their training has resulted, with attendant higher job satisfaction, longer-term employment, higher-quality service, and higher productivity.

APPLICATION OF TECHNOLOGY

Factory automation, computer-controlled machine tools, and robotics are catching all the attention today, even though Theodore Levitt's description of the french fry machine at McDonald's[15] more graphically shows the application of technology to service operations. New technologies now being developed and implemented promise to have a much greater impact on productivity in certain of the service industries than factory automation is having on manufacturing.

Felix Rohatyn, the well-known investment banker who serves on the boards of eight major corporations and played a major role in restructuring the finances of New York City, describes Schlumberger, the world's largest supplier of oil exploration services, in this way:

> By the standard of profit margins, return on investment, compound growth rate, of remaining ahead in the state of the art technically and having an efficient management structure, over the last 20 years—until the recent drastic change in the energy environment—Schlumberger might well have been the single best business in the world.[16]

True, the company hires the best engineers it can find to staff its more than 2,000 field exploration teams that collect and process data indicating the best drilling strategies and likelihood of success at various petroleum drilling sites. But other competitors have access to the same skilled engineers as Schlumberger.

Schlumberger has gained and maintained its competitive advantage by developing and employing the latest technology to leverage the efforts of its field representatives. The company's equipment charts electric current as it encounters various kinds of rock, water, and oil. By comparing the actual current coursing through the earth with records showing the electrical resistivity of each substance, an engineer can produce what amounts to an X-ray of an oil well. Assuming, of course, that he or she knows how to read and interpret the data.

Even without a patent on the basic process, Schlumberger continues to maintain a 70 percent share of the multibillion-dollar-oil-well "logging" business because of its devotion to developing the most advanced technology that can improve the odds of an accurate test by only a small amount. However, a small improvement is worth a great deal to a company investing up to $10,000 per day in an exploration effort.

The entire specialty retailing industry is undergoing a remarkable change made possible by communications and computing. Firms that have understood its potential have been able to develop significant competitive advantage. B. Dalton, the book-retailing subsidiary of Dayton-Hudson, has developed what is recognized as a highly effective inventory control system at several hundred retail sites in a business beset with problems of managing thousands of units of sometimes highly perishable inventory.

The wholesaling of grocery products, once thought to be outmoded by the growth of supermarket chains, has been changed dramatically in recent years by technology. The management of one of the most successful grocery wholesalers, Super Valu, now claims to be able to make an independently owned supermarket as efficient and productive as a chain competitor of equal size, primarily through the use of several computer-oriented analytic devices. Regarded as a "retail support company" by its leadership, Super Valu achieves its goals by concentrating on its own warehouses and on its retailers' stores. At the former, industrial engineering and advanced computer modeling are used to increase warehouse utilization and throughput as well as worker productivity. A computer simulator has been programmed to analyze the productivity and storage capacity of various warehouse arrangements. Changing sales patterns can trigger Super Valu's warehouse layouts to be "changed" ("reset") roughly once per month, compared to once per year for some of its competitors.

Super Valu supports its independent retailers through the development and use of a SLASH (Site Location Analysis Strategy Heuristic) program to help them select the proper store location. A computer-aided design system permits architects to try out over 100 store plans on a CRT screen. And the company has been putting in place programs to capitalize on the inventory data being made available by the electronic price scanning devices being installed by Super Valu's retailer customers. Super Valu and its retail customers have been recording phenomenal growth in an industry generally regarded as mature.[17]

The management of Federal Express has combined high tech with high touch (high personal contact) to achieve productivity targets while catering to customers' expectations that their overnight package or letter shipments are receiving personal attention. On the high tech side, the company planes are equipped with Magic Window, a radar computer imaging device that permits pilots to see through fog, thereby increasing shipment dependability. The company's hand-held digital-assisted dispatch system (DADS) provides driver contact with the dispatcher at all times. Orders are entered and shipments tracked on COSMOS, a system allowing personnel to build a real-time, on-line data base to track shipments moving through the system. A recent count indicated that the company had installed more than 10,000 on-line terminals in company and customer facilities and more than 7,000 communication terminals in its 10,000 radio-dispatched company vans, all intended to increase productivity and level of service for package delivery. At the same time, the company's ZAP Mail is handled via satellite communication and laser printers.

The company employs 500 agents to accept up to 120,000 incoming orders during the peak hours of 2:00 to 4:00 P.M. And COSMOS, operating in tandem with computerized telecommunications systems, allows those agents to answer incoming calls, according to one Federal Express executive, "within three rings—and by someone who immediately knows you are 'located on the second floor,' ask for Joe."[18]

Banking has not been the same since the introduction of even the simplest automatic teller machine (ATM) in 1970 in Valdosta, Georgia. Wells Fargo Bank "has been able to cut 700 people from its work force of 8,000 and close thirty of its 400 California branches in two years by installing automated teller machines."[19] More recently, ATMs have been supplemented with more advanced models capable of doubling the productivity of tellers by supplying the customer with more accurate information faster.

All this equipment has been linked to computer-supported management information systems that have changed the face of bank management as well. ATMs have enabled banks to extend their services beyond their premises, literally into other high-traffic locations such as air terminals, supermarkets, and shopping centers. In the process, of course, they have brought into question the larger matters of competition and the regulation of the entire industry, particularly that part of regulation that depends on the definition of a bank branch. But they have enabled technological leaders among banks to gather a larger share of the business in a particular market and to channel it into a more efficient delivery system whose productivity is enhanced by increased volume.

INVOLVING THE CUSTOMER

The ATM may represent a superior application of technology in increasing productivity, but it would not have been successful unless customers were willing to become involved in the service delivery process itself. Customers have proved quite willing to carry out part of the service delivery process if it can be shown to be profitable, convenient, sociable, or just plain fun. A number of successful service firms have capitalized on this.

Direct dialing of telephones reduces the costs of connecting callers by 80 percent. But since none of that savings initially could be passed on to the individual for each call dialed, it was necessary to prove to the customer that it was time-saving. It took longer, but it worked.

Some consumers go to shopping centers rather than having goods delivered to their homes by a shopping service because they enjoy being with other people. They will carry their own baggage on board aircraft to enjoy the peace of mind of knowing where it is.

More insurance is being sold by telephone to customers who are willing to inform themselves about alternatives before placing a telephone order. A vigorous and growing discount investment brokerage service has captured more than 30 percent of the U.S. brokerage business by catering to people who are willing to collect their own information about investments and need only an inexpensive transaction service. Health maintenance organizations (HMOs) are encouraging individuals to take greater responsibility for their physical well-being. We put ZIP codes on envelopes and pump our own gas. Those services are being made more productive in the process.

As Christopher Lovelock and Robert Young have pointed out, customer involvement has not been easily achieved. The firms most successful in encouraging customer participation have concentrated on developing customer trust or capitalizing on the trust that a customer holds for the server, understanding customers' habits, pretesting new procedures and equipment, understanding customers' motivations and behavior, teaching customers how to use service innovations in a nonthreatening way, promoting the benefits and stimulating trial, and monitoring and evaluating the performance of the innovation.[20]

Where these steps are taken, more, not all, customers can be involved without perceiving a serious deterioration in service. Many who actually perceive improvements in service quality are customers who, as Lovelock and Young have suggested, may have time on their hands while waiting for service, may feel it unnecessary or even undesirable for personal contact in the process, ask questions unnecessarily because they are ill-informed, are not interested in personal service extras, or are genuinely interested in the service delivery process.[21]

What about the others? Provisions are made for them through back-up services such as telephone operators, personal-service bank branches, and full-service pumps at filling stations. But as a well-conceived, self-service concept takes hold, the numbers of nonparticipants have dwindled steadily, contributing to company and industry productivity.

CHAPTER SIX

Operating Strategy
Barriers to Entry

Generalizations about the service sector nearly always are proved wrong because the industries are so diverse. This is especially true of barriers to entry, which generally are assumed to range from near-absolute for the utility industry—one of the last operated under the theory of the natural monopoly whereby government bars entry—to very low barriers for those entering the trucking and the fast-food business.

Even so, a senior executive of Roadway Express, the largest intercity highway carrier of general freight, might say that the entry fee for carriers providing national service is so high that it represents an effective barrier to entry. Roadway's business is simply not affected by how many individuals buy and sell trucks every day as they enter and leave the industry. In contrast, economies of scale are so easy to attain in a given market in the fast-food business that they are low-entry barriers, representing a competitive problem even for the local franchise of a firm as large as McDonald's.

Barriers to entry are changing even in the utilities industry. Many firms have newly entered the power-generating business under the impetus of high cost-increases, thanks to current regulations that not only permit individuals and organizations to generate their own power but also require local utilities to buy the excess power they generate. Economic incentives and a guaranteed market have once again confused theory.

Barriers to entry provide effective forms of competitive advantage, particularly if they are earned and require constant maintenance. When government provides them, they can become a narcotic, often of little positive benefit to the development of effective management, and they can produce terrible withdrawal pains when removed or reduced.

The literature on barriers to entry is voluminous and relevant for most service industries. Michael Porter, for example, suggests that important sources of such barriers are high economies of scale, high product differentiation, high capital requirements for entry, high customer switching costs, difficulty of access to distribution channels, cost advantages independent of scale (including those derived from proprietary product technology, favorable access to raw materials, favorable locations, government subsidies, and learning or experience curve effects), and government policy.[1] Several of these have already been discussed. This chapter will concentrate on phenomena of particular importance to service industries, phenomena that are shared with relatively few manufacturing enterprises.

ECONOMIES OF SCALE

Economies of or returns to scale are defined by Porter as "declines in unit costs of a service as the absolute volume *per* [any calendar] *period* increases."[2] They are found in service industries at the level of the product, the business, or the company. They are directly associated with the *joint costs* that predominate in many service businesses, those costs that could not be reduced if a product or business were eliminated.

Many service businesses require much more capacity than is needed to satisfy all but peak demand. An airline typically operates at 55 to 60 percent of capacity, a range so low that it would bankrupt most manufacturing firms. Over a 70 percent utilization rate, many airline passengers begin to notice a marked deterioration of good service in relation to their expectations. Scheduling decisions are made no more frequently than every three months or so, yet every passenger that can be added to a scheduled flight yields nearly as much profit as revenue. Joint costs at the unit level—an entire plane—are extremely high in this business, placing a premium on efforts to match equipment and capacity to market demands and to entice as many potential passengers as possible. Other industries that have difficulty in adjusting capacity, especially reducing it, encounter the same problem.

In contrast, the basic unit of capacity in the insurance industry is the sales representative. The level of investment in that representative is relatively low. Since the costs of new business vary somewhat with each additional unit of sale, a sales rep is rewarded on commission rather than salary. The penalties and difficulties of cutting back on capacity are therefore not as great in insurance as in air transport. In bad times, the capacity adjusts itself in natural, sometimes favorable ways; the least established, least effective sales reps may be the most likely to leave of their own accord. The challenge in the insurance business is to discourage the most promising sales talent from leaving.

Economies of scale may vary from one aspect of the business to another. Returns are limited in the marketing arms of many insurance companies, but those associated with data-processing, actuarial, and investment functions may be much greater. Here again, the minimum capability needed to run the business may have excess capacity available when the volume of business increases.

Economies of scale depend upon the way in which capacity must be added and upon the strategy adopted for managing that capacity. The minimum-sized addition of an extra aircraft to an airline creates a smaller increment of capacity than the addition of a new, acceptably efficient, power-generating plant to a utility's operation. Both represent much larger stepwise additions to capacity than does the hiring of an additional sales rep in an insurance company. But these actions create interim opportunities for achieving economies of scale in direct proportion to the importance of the stepwise addition of capacity.

Capacity management may follow one of several strategies: "level," set at some proportion (up to 100 percent or more) of peak load; or "chase," with capacity adjusted to demand as the latter becomes known or can be projected. The costs of level strategies are largely fixed, allowing for large economies of scale through increased off-peak demand. The costs of chase strategies vary more widely with volume. Large personnel costs of training and severance, or high equipment costs for short-term rental, sometimes on relatively short notice, are common.

RELATIONSHIPS BETWEEN SHARE OF SERVICE OFFERED AND SHARE OF MARKET

The share of service offered in certain service industries has cumulative effects on the share of market. That is, as the share of one company's service increases the total of service offered by all competitors, the company's share of market increases faster at certain points in the relationship. This is called the "S-curve" effect, shown in Figure 6-1. William Fruhan has documented it for the airline industry.[3]

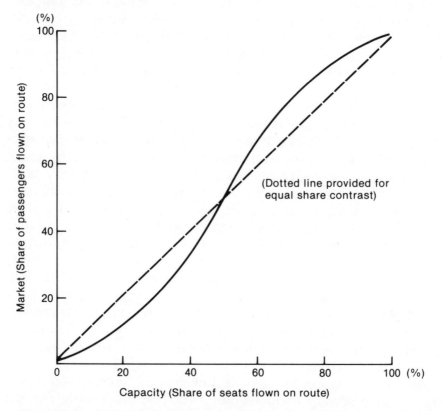

Adapted from: William E. Fruhan, Jr., *The Fight for Competitive Advantage: A Study of the United States Domestic Trunk Carrier*. Boston: Division of Research, Harvard Business School, 1972, 127. Used with permission.

[a]The diagram should be read as follows: By flying 20% of all seats flown on a route on which its competitor flies 80% of the seats, an airline may expect to attract only 10% of the total passengers.

Figure 6-1
The "S-Curve" Effect in the Airline Industry: Market Share vs. Capacity Share on a Two-Carrier Route[a]

The "S-curve" is thought to typify services in which: one firm's product (seats leaving at desired departure times) is difficult to differentiate from another's; capacity must be added in significant increments (whole airplanes); and the customer's perception of the level of service available is related directly to the quantity of desired capacity made available. These conditions apply wherever a premium is placed on proximity to the service, and thus to businesses as diverse as equipment repair, banking, and convenience retailing.

The more service representatives per computer in a given locale in relation to competition, the faster the relative response to service calls, the higher the comparative level of service perceived by the customer, and the greater the probabilities a computer manufacturer may realize the next sale of service or, more importantly, equipment. In other words, the share of incremental market the company might enjoy increases.

The effect of the "S-curve" on industry behavior can be profound. It creates an incentive to add capacity to build market share, particularly for firms operating at or near the point of positive inflection (where market share increases faster than share of service offered). With all firms operating on a specific airline route, striving to reach and exceed the point of positive inflection, the inevitable result is overcapacity and inefficient operations for the industry as a whole. Short of outright collusion or industry agreements, such as airline pooling (or schedule and capacity sharing) that have been organized in Europe, there is no clear way out. The most effective antidote appears to be raising levels of service or lowering prices.

Because Singapore Airlines' labor costs are low, it has been able to offer significantly lower rates on its service to the Far East. On the long flight segments where service counts, it has used its low wages to employ up to four more cabin attendants, featured high-quality cuisine and cabin service, and operated the newest fleet of aircraft of any major airline. Its load factors (percentage of seats flown full) have exceeded 70 percent when its major competitors were flying at 60 percent or less in an industry where one percentage point of load factor makes a big difference. Singapore has achieved these advantages without offering more seats on a given route than its competition.[4]

Continental Airlines, by obtaining important union concessions during a period of bankruptcy, has developed the same low-labor cost advantage in its largely U.S. operation. It has chosen to use this advantage to offer full service and significantly lower fares and to achieve much higher load factors (percentage of filled seats) than its major competitors.

DEVELOPMENT OF SWITCHING COSTS

By increasing switching costs to their customers, other service competitors have attempted to reduce the effects of the S-curve and still achieve competitive advantage. An investment broker who arranges a customer's account to handle securities trading, savings, and checking capabilities and then supervises it with some understanding of the customer's background, needs, and preferences, can commit a customer so fully that it would require a major effort for the client to change brokers. Similarly, loans may include penalty clauses for early payment; frequent-user clubs encourage travelers to concentrate their patronage with one airline, hotel, and auto rental agency; and insurance policies have no cash value until they have been in effect for several years.

NETWORK EFFECTS

Network effects are important opportunities for gaining competitive advantage in industries in which the basic service consists of linking buyers, sellers, and third parties. That includes transportation and travel, communications, credit card services, banking, power generation, and distribution.

First, networks raise the cost of entry to a level that few potential competitors can or will pay. Unless a newcomer is willing to invest in facilities at two or more "nodes" as well as in the means to connect them—whether by wire, trucks, or some type of agreement—entry is discouraged.

More important for competitive strategy, network-oriented services usually are enhanced by expanding the network. Its facilities are more widely used if the expansion enhances its value to customers. Shortly after deregulation of the trucking industry, no more than ten of the larger companies (out of roughly 16,000 truckers under Interstate Commerce Commission regulation) set out to create a nationwide network of terminals and routes by programming massive investments over a period of several years. Where customer loyalty, switching costs, or habit patterns are dominant, the firm making the early investment in a network may enjoy a long-term competitive advantage over the newcomer.

Once a customer franchise is built through network enhancement, it may be difficult to displace. The competitive dynamics of the U.S. banking industry illustrates the point well. In the 1960s, two major bank credit-card-systems were initiated to allow bank customers to charge purchases from retailers. The two systems, which eventually became known as MasterCard and VISA, signed up retailers who would accept the cards, while the member banks who owned a share in one of the two systems distributed cards to their customers. The service delivered by each system depends on the size of the network established in a region relevant to cardholders. Beginning in the 1980s, VISA has been the more aggressive of the two organizations, developing a worldwide network of about 50,000 retailers, some 50 million cardholders, and about 60 percent of the volume shared by both services. VISA has grown far beyond the bounds its 15,000 bank-owners envisioned for it.[5]

Recently, a different form of competition to these bank cards has arisen. In 1981 Merrill Lynch established its Cash Management Account (CMA), allowing a customer to maintain an investment account and to have unused funds automatically placed in a high interest-bearing money market fund and to make charges against the account by check or credit card. Innovative Banc One of Columbus, Ohio, came forth with a proposal to provide checks and its VISA card in exchange for the data-processing business associated with the funds transfer. The bank-owners of VISA were thus faced overnight with a nonbank competitor offering a range of bank-like services using the VISA card nationally, something they were prohibited by law from doing. Through their money market funds, "nonbank-banks" such as Merrill Lynch had already siphoned off $185 billion in deposits from banks and thrift institutions.

To avert regulation prohibiting interstate banking and to meet the new competition, bankers organized. They created national networks by connecting their automated teller machines, allowing their customers access to all ATMs in the network through the use of a debit card, and by providing cash on demand through a direct debit to a cardholder's bank account. In a period of several years, most banks have become affiliated with one of these networks, operating alongside VISA and MasterCard. VISA's response has been to announce the development of a worldwide network of

ATMs, with plans for at least 8,000 machines in several dozen countries by the end of 1986.[6]

VISA's announcement was received with something less than full enthusiasm by its owners, many of whom joined national networks constructed to preclude direct competitors in a major market from belonging to the same network. Given VISA's network of retail establishments, the consumer franchise of its name and card, and the international reach it provides, its member banks will find it difficult not to tie themselves to the network, thus destroying much of the competitive uniqueness of their own ATM networks. The power of services provided by VISA's networks may well shield it from the competition of its owners, some of whom now feel they have created a monster (VISA) they cannot control.

THE DATA BASE AND INFORMATION TECHNOLOGY AS STRATEGIC WEAPONS

The most valuable assets that many service firms possess do not even appear on their balance sheets. They are the data-base and associated-information technologies. Both cost a great deal to assemble and maintain, and together they offer a variety of opportunities both for exploring the needs of customers whose profiles a data base may contain and for developing new services to meet those needs.

Small firms can deploy these powerful barriers to entry as well. American Home Shield, a company providing service contracts for electrical, plumbing, and heating systems in individual homes, has used the data base it constructed to improve its service, reduce the inventories of parts it holds, and learn as much as anyone in the United States about performance patterns of equipment supplied by major manufacturers. While widening its competitive advantage in its service regions, American Home Shield is now considering other services that can benefit both homeowners and manufacturers who utilize its data base.[7]

American Airlines has devised a potent competitive device. It uses its data base of airline operating information in conjunction with its highly regarded SABRE computerized reservation system and the largest network of proprietary computer terminals in travel agencies. American and United supplied nearly 80 percent of all such terminals in 1982. The flight information such terminals display influences flight selection in favor of the airline sponsoring the terminal. Other airlines whose schedules are shown along with American's and United's have charged that the sponsoring airline lists its flight first in a particular time slot. Such systems may also list only the "host" airline's flights as departing shortly before the time requested by the traveler, who then decides to leave earlier to catch a more direct flight. A carrier that books through reservations terminals can influence in its favor up to 20 percent of the business in geographical areas where it offers extensive services. In an industry in which two of ten major competitors control nearly 80 percent of travel agency reservations terminals, the data base and its presentation are considered a distinct competitive advantage.[8]

Dun & Bradstreet's $1.6 billion business is centered on its data base, a file of credit information describing businesses in thirty countries. It is being steadily extended through development and merger. Its new product development effort has been producing services that were not in existence three years earlier but that now yield 10 percent of the company's total volume. They all use the same data base, presenting information packaged in different forms to the same or new customers. While the company's competitors use much smaller, focused data bases and services, a potential competitor would have to spend an estimated $1 billion just to duplicate Dun & Bradstreet's—a figure nearly half of Dun & Bradstreet's own net asset value.

On an even larger scale, the number of U.S. households in which people hold Sears, Roebuck and Co.'s credit cards has been estimated at 60 million, half of which actively use them, making Sears' card the most widely held in the world. The names and addresses of its cardholders alone are a major asset, but they become much more valuable with additional information about purchase and payment patterns. Other financial institutions therefore found it difficult to ignore Sears' acquisitions of an investment banking firm, Dean Witter & Company, a leading real estate brokerage firm, savings and loan companies, and a bank, all now combined with its long-standing Allstate property, casualty, and life insurance business. Sears could soon develop a debit card, begin placing automatic teller machines in its stores, and make a significant move into secured and unsecured lending. It could, in short, be acting like a bank—a big one. Almost overnight, Sears has put together one of the potentially most profitable of all U.S.

financial institutions in spite of initial profit declines incurred by Dean Witter.

The potential for using Sears' data base in Dean Witter's investment brokerage business was described in the somewhat surprising results of a consultant study, released in 1981:

> Possession of Sears' cards increases as family incomes rise. Among households with more than $36,000 in annual income, the study found that 70% had Sears cards. Among households with net worth of more than $500,000, 76% had Sears cards. And among all brokerage house customers, 62% had Sears cards, while 73% of stock market investors making transactions worth $25,000 or more per year also carry the card. "Even Sears was surprised" by the study, says a consultant close to the company. "They thought they were more blue-collar than they are."
>
> Dean Witter's Melton, in a letter to his employees praising the merger, added that the retailer has done a study of its own showing that 625,000 regular Sears merchandise customers would consider opening a new account with a brokerage firm associated with Sears. That many new clients would about double Dean Witter's present roster.[9]

Sears recently announced that it is rapidly expanding the number of financial service centers located in its stores. It is simply putting its largest hidden asset to work.

Warren McFarlan has pointed out that information technologies not only provide access to the riches of a collected data base, but they can also change the balance of power in supplier-customer relationships and the very basis of competition itself.[10] Top managements of firms as diverse as American Home Shield, American Airlines, Dun & Bradstreet, and Sears appreciate the resource and are willing to invest for long-term competitive advantage.

The ability of service firms to take full advantage of the vast amounts of potentially useful information stored in their data bases may well depend on the manner in which they use it in the short run. Increasingly frequent reports of leaks of personal credit information and of computer theft of names, addresses, and credit card numbers have raised public concern about the adequacy of privacy laws. Firms relying heavily on such data will find it in their best interests to establish guidelines for the responsible use of stored personal data which might well become the basis for whatever regulation is finally proposed. The best interests of service firms may be served by pushing for positive legislation of this type.

CHAPTER SEVEN

People and the Service Culture

On December 15, 1982, more than 90 percent of Delta Airlines' employees chipped in $30 million and presented the company with a Boeing 767, named *The Spirit of Delta*. The fund for the plane was started by three stewardesses who, in spite of top management's reticence, felt that something should be done as a sign of general appreciation for a pay raise given at a time of general industry difficulty. In 1984, the leadership of the seventeen unions making up the Railway Labor Executives Association encouraged Bill Marriott, Jr., to bid for the purchase of the government-owned Conrail against several other bidders, including themselves. The unions' labor financial advisor "felt that the option of having two offers that rail labor liked strengthened his position."[1] At Wal-Mart, one of the fastest-growing and most profitable of all discount general merchandise retailers, senior managers have for some time worn buttons proclaiming, "We Care About Our People."

Are these events public relations gimmicks dreamed up by the manipulative managements of these companies? Hardly. They are sincere expressions of the high regard in which the managements of these companies hold their employees. By putting employees first, they encourage positive attitudes that spill over into relations with customers. The result is financial success for shareholders as well.

117

"People are our most important asset" would head the hypothetical list of clichés uttered by managers and printed in annual reports. It comes up so often that we tend to take it for granted, and its omission is the first step toward the decline of any people-intensive business. In many service industries in which people may be a firm's only significant asset, it may also be difficult to build a product backlog as a buffer against potential strikes. Thus, there is an additional economic incentive for maintaining positive manager–employee relationships.[2]

The most successful performers in service industries have learned something else of great significance for most manufacturers: how to coordinate operating and marketing efforts. Because their operations and marketing are often embodied in the same person at the point of service delivery, leading service firms are at the forefront of experimentation with new types of organization and management of human resources.

ORGANIZATION

Profiles of successful service firms display common management themes: they are lean at the top, they have a limited hierarchy, and they coordinate marketing and operations at low levels in the organization.

LEAN AT THE TOP

Senior executive groups are usually composed of no more than a handful of people. There are few or no staff members at surprisingly small corporate headquarters offices. Members of top management are frequently interchangeable, sharing similar responsibilities and able to fill in where needed. There is a tendency to work through profit centers created among small groups of first-level employees, regardless of the amount of discretion they are allowed in performing their jobs. (These are variations on the general theme of decentralization.) And a kind of puritanical spirit among top managers works against a "star" system of high salaries or a focus on only one or two senior executives.

At Delta, in an industry whose early pioneers were some of the best-known and most flamboyant managers anywhere, the company is run by nine senior executives whose names most other senior executives in the airline industry would be hard-pressed to recall. With Delta's aviation pioneer, C. W. Woolman, in failing health, a cadre of senior managers gradually took over and shared his responsibilities among themselves. According to one account, "They learned to manage by teamwork and consensus."[3] Averaging more than twenty-five years' experience among them, they have been operating like a team ever since, capable of assuming each other's duties when necessary.

Marriott is headed by a person with a well-known name, but Bill Marriott, Jr., very successfully lives down that possible handicap with his employees. Many of his days away from the office, 180 in a recent year, are spent talking with employees about their jobs, inspecting properties, or visiting the sites of new facilities, eyeing design details.[4]

One observer has described Wal-Mart's headquarters as a somewhat empty warehouse.[5] Senior managers, what few there are, spend a great deal of their time in Wal-Mart's eleven-state service areas, "leading local cheerleading squads at new store openings, scouting out competing K Mart stores, and conducting soul-searching sessions with employees."[6]

Schlumberger's $6 billion business in oil field services and related activities is run on a worldwide basis with a corporate headquarters staff of 150, including secretaries, in the company's New York and Paris offices. In 1980 when Schlumberger acquired Fairchild Camera & Instrument Corporation, a semiconductor chip manufacturer with sales approaching $1 billion per year, it immediately reduced Fairchild's corporate staff by two-thirds: from 600 to 200 people. The action in Schlumberger's wireline service is in the more remote parts of some seventy-five countries, where each of its more than 2,000 businesses is run by a field engineer vith one truck, a crew of two, and equipment worth more than $1 million. "You're the final word on that location," says Bill McGovern, a recruiting engineer who has been in the field three years, "and it's your responsibility." Like McGovern, many engineers go on to higher posts.[7] Independence and self-reliance are qualities the company looks for in new recruits, because it promotes managers from its internal ranks.

Super Valu, a $5-billion grocery wholesaler high on the "best performers" list of service firms, has only fifteen corporate officers in its Minneapolis headquarters.[8]

Extensive decentralization does not mean that these organizations approach anarchy. While Marriott's hotel managers have profit responsibilities and considerable discretion in developing their individual properties,

> the company became one of the industry's most efficient by applying a tightly centralized system of policies, procedures, and controls to the slightest operational detail. Every job has a manual that breaks down the work into a mind-boggling number of steps. A hotel maid, for instance, has 66 things to do in cleaning up a room, from dusting the tops of all pictures (Step No. 7) to making sure the telephone books and Bibles are in good, neat condition (Step No. 37). "The more the system works like the Army," says Marriott, "the better."[9]

When a delivery system works like the army, managers and non-managers alike spend less time correcting faults and more time engaging in activities designed to improve rapport with customers in services requiring a high degree of customer contact. The result is more volume and profit for a decentralized, high fixed-cost operation.

At Scandinavian Airline System, the turnaround of the company's performance was recently accomplished under the leadership of Jan Carlzon, who reduced corporate overhead by $23 million per year and who divided the company into profit centers ranging in size from an airline division down to the London–Stockholm route. Here:

> a route manager is a virtual entrepreneur, free to decide the time and number of flights between two cities—contingent on the approval of the governments involved. He leases airplanes and flight crews from other divisions.[10]

LIMITED HIERARCHY

Successful service firms are often "lean organizations" with few levels of jobs. The motive is just as likely to preserve communication channels and a strong customer orientation as well as cost control. People Express, one of the first low-fare offspring of the deregulation of the passenger airline industry in the United States, began operations in 1981. In many ways the airline has been an exercise in the management of human resources. People Express reflects the views of its founder, Donald Burr: "I guess the single predominant reason that I cared about starting a new company was to try to develop a better way for people to work together."[11]

Convinced that a complex hierarchy was at cross-purposes with this philosophy, Burr and his associates founded their firm with an organization that included only three levels: Seven managing officers had eight general managers reporting to them and then there was everyone else. Everyone at People occupies positions as flight managers (pilots), maintenance managers (supervisors of People's maintenance contracts), and customer service managers (everyone performing passenger-related tasks on the ground and in the plane). Other jobs are performed by contractors.

A lack of hierarchy can imply a lack of supervisory capability in the traditional sense; but at People employees are selected, trained, and assigned for work in three- or four-person work groups that perform much of their own supervision and control.

COORDINATION OF OPERATIONS AND MARKETING

Firms providing high-contact, on-line services in which it is difficult to "buffer" the customer from the server are most sensitive to the need for effective coordination between operations and marketing management. Unlike most manufacturing firms and other off-line services, their products are marketed and produced simultaneously. Rather than view this as a handicap, their managements have pioneeered ways to foster much-needed coordination at the lowest possible levels in their organizations.

Manufacturing firms most often are organized according to the traditional view that marketing and manufacturing functions should be separate and equal, coordinated at relatively high levels. In high-contact service industries one function is more often subordinated to the other. Because the local manager in a multisite operation is usually given responsibilty for both functions and reports through the operations function, marketing is seen as subordinated to, and given less emphasis than, operations.[12]

While this view may be applicable to manufacturing in which functions can be buffered from one another, a study of 360 manufacturing and service firms provides a somewhat different picture. Traditional marketing activities such as product/service development, pricing, advertising, and promotion management are indeed performed in service firms, but they are performed outside the marketing function more often than in manufacturing firms. The study's authors concluded that, contrary to popular belief, service firms place just as much importance on marketing research as do manufacturing firms.[13]

The emphasis in service firms has been on integrating operations and marketing, regardless of reporting relationships. Where integration is most important, it has been achieved at much lower levels than in most manufacturing organizations. More than 90 percent of all field managers in four multisite service firms surveyed in one study indicated they were responsible for operations, personnel, and marketing; they could not distinguish easily in importance between these responsibilities; and they devoted significant proportions of their time to all three.[14]

Even when operations are buffered from the field in service organizations, innovative steps may be taken to break down traditional functional barriers. Several years ago at Chase Manhattan Bank N.A., a senior executive was given responsibility for a significant part of both communications and operations associated with international business. The purpose was to improve the quality of the bank's nonloan products, to improve the bank's external communications and customer services, and to make production "back-room" operations more market-based. In the highly visible "product" of international money transfer, functional and psychological barriers arose between the account relationship manager in the field and operations management at headquarters. The resulting lack of cross-functional knowledge created a large backlog of inquiries and errors and a breakdown in the morale of the operations group.

A study of the situation suggested that only about one-third of all inquiries could be attributed to operational errors at Chase and that marketing personnel had little idea what operations personnel could offer to the bank's customers. As a result, backlogged errors were resolved after being traced to their sources, often a correspondent bank. A campaign was launched to improve the morale of operations personnel around the theme, "We make it happen." A new organizational group called the "Customer Mobile Unit" was formed and staffed with the most experienced international operations people in the bank. Its primary purpose was to make on-site visits to Chase customers to help resolve problems and insure mutually smooth operations. Most important, reporting relationships were revised to require production managers to report to both the account relationship manager and the head of operations, thus coordinating the organization functionally.[15]

PERSONNEL POLICIES

The concept of "family" pervades many of the most successful service companies. People hired are not simply employees or workers but are "crew members" at McDonald's and "cast members" at Disney Productions, operators of Disneyland and other entertainment businesses. And at Delta Airlines, the firm emphasizes in its various activities the term "Family Feeling." Other policies associated with the concept of family are careful employee selection, long-term employment, promotion from within, and a strong emphasis on personal development with special attention given to job assignment.

EMPLOYEE SELECTION

One person can regard a job in food service as a boring, repetitive task, while another can see the same job as offering an endless variety of opportunities to meet and interact with people. Research suggests that some of the employee attributes of success in high-contact ("on-line") service situations include flexibility, tolerance for ambiguity, the ability to monitor and change behavior during the service encounter, and empathy with customers.[16] The last attribute was found in one study to be more important than age, education, sales-related knowledge, sales training, and intelligence.[17] Unfortunately, less appears to be known about how to select people possessing these qualifications. A remarkably small number of validated tests has produced modest results.[18] Even situational interviews can yield as good a set of results.[19] One group of researchers in 1984 concluded, "We could find no existing measures that adequately assess service orientation."[20]

Fortunately, there is a reasonable amount of data to suggest that people with characteristics required for effective performance in high-contact service jobs gravitate toward these jobs.[21] Benjamin Schneider has concluded that most employees in such jobs are self-motivated to provide what they believe is good customer service, but they complain that management frustrates their desires to give good service.[22] Successful service firms capitalize on these desires.

At People Express, Lori Dubose, then managing officer of the company's personnel as well as of in-flight functions, faced a particularly difficult challenge in selection. In addition to the many qualities sought by all airlines for their personnel, Dubose and her recruiters had to find people (even pilots) capable of functioning independently, wanting to develop personally, willing to perform multiple tasks, interested in achieving and purchasing company stock as a condition of permanent employment, able to collaborate with others, and comfortable with the company's horizontal structure. Initially People hired one out of every 100 applicants. This care was important because of another company policy: all permanent positions at People carry the security of lifetime employment, a variation on a feature found in many successful service firms.

LONG-TERM EMPLOYMENT

Delta has not laid off or even furloughed a single full-time employee for economic reasons in more than twenty-five years. Although the strike of the Air Traffic Controllers in 1981 forced the firm to cut back significantly on its operations, it redeployed temporarily displaced pilots and others to other jobs, including selling tickets, loading cargo, and cleaning airplanes. David C. Garrett, Jr., Delta's president and chief executive officer, said, "Sure, that was a blow to the size of their paychecks, especially in the case of the pilots, but they still got paychecks and they kept their seniority and all their medical benefits."[23] This redeployment was possible largely because Delta had carefully developed a sense of teamwork among its employees, and it had one of the most generous benefit plans in U.S. industry (reflecting the attitude of the founder that "you protect the family"). The company is also the least unionized of the major airlines, and, perhaps most important, has an implied policy of lifetime employment.

PROMOTION FROM WITHIN

In contrast to Delta, United Parcel Service is the largest single employer of members of the International Brotherhood of Teamsters and has more than 85,000 people on its payroll. Its relationships with its drivers have been strained at times. The company has been struck more than once. UPS demands a great deal from its drivers, supervises them closely, and applies close controls; but its wages average more than $14 an hour, high for local drivers, and it holds out the opportunity for the more successful drivers to become supervisors, each entrusted with the supervision of other drivers and routes. Supervisors immediately become eligible to purchase the company's stock, a highly valued and valuable asset through the years. And, of course, they enter the stream of future managers, nearly all of whom are promoted from within. Ronald Carey, president of Teamsters Local 804 in Long Island City, New York, has said that "if UPS announced it had 1,000 openings for drivers tomorrow, there would be 100,000 applicants."[24]

PERSONAL DEVELOPMENT

The Marriott Corporation maintains a number of related programs to encourage the development of its employees. One, called Individual Development (ID), is designed to teach necessary skills and technical information to new managers in a consistent way, critically important to service companies operating geographically dispersed units. A second, Management Training, requires every member of the company's middle management to attend one management development session per year.

Perhaps the most interesting is the third program, Career Progression, for which employees must request consideration. It is intended to provide nonsupervisory employees with an opportunity to take on positions of increasing skill, responsibility, and pay, with possible entry into management. Employees with good attitudes, aptitudes, and Marriott work history are accepted. With a personnel supervisor, each then works out an individual 90-day program of orientation, general training, and advanced training aimed at promotion when an opening occurs in the targeted position. As the brochure describing this program explains: "Career progression takes only 90 days to complete. It's your program, designed to give you the chance to earn a better job for more pay, and you are the only one who's going to make it work." The booklet advises that, on promotion: "Do your best and think about training for the next job."[25]

Contrast this program with Burstiner's findings that newly hired salespeople in department stores often receive twelve times as much training in store policies and cash register operation as they receive in selling.[26]

ASSIGNMENT

Personal job assignments and their progression over time are an important contribution to personal development in any firm. They take on added significance in services where there is a heavy reliance on people; and they are critical in firms, most often professional service firms, in which the person delivering the service must tailor it to a customer's needs and exhibit a high degree of skill and judgment in doing so.

The client of the management consultant, advertising agency, or architectural firm is paying for the highest level of expertise available and often desires the server to have previous experience in the client's industry. The professional service firm, for its part, seeks to leverage the time of its most highly skilled representatives with the time of others to achieve the desired "multiple" (margin) at a reasonable price to the client. It may seek to rotate its personnel periodically from client to client and even from industry to industry, to develop people, multiply their contacts with partners in the firm who eventually will have to rule on their suitability for partnership, and deter clients and employees from creating too strong a set of ties. This rotation may be opposed by both clients and more senior project leaders in the service firm. The young professional may be torn between the desire to develop through a diversity of assignments and the desire to maintain continuity in both client relationships and internal working relationships within the firm.

Thus, the job of managing assignments requires playing off many considerations against one another. In firms achieving the greatest success, one member of the firm's management may oversee the assignment process, so critical that it may receive the attention of a senior partner, often on a rotating basis. Although project leaders may request associates they would like to have working with them, the final decision often remains with the assignment manager (hence, the importance of a senior partner in the role). The process is managed from a set of clearly stated (but often flexibly interpreted) guidelines and involves frequent consultation between the assignment manager, senior partners as a group, project leaders, and younger associates.

Variety in assignments is central to personal development in other types of service firms as well. For example, at People Express rotation or cross-utilization in jobs can be expected by the company's personnel as frequently as every month. Everyone, including managing officers, regularly exchanges line and staff jobs, inflight and ground jobs. While this policy has proved troublesome to some, particularly with the recent growth of the company, People's management has regarded it as well worth the short-term expense and inconvenience.

MOTIVATION

If we can believe the message of many leading service firms, motivation starts not with compensation but with effective communication. In a service firm, internal communication among employees is often more important than the more visible external communication with customers. This includes clear communication of job expectation, joint goal-setting by employees and their supervisors, straightforward measurement and appraisal of results, and follow-up to help people improve through positive reinforcement and personal development. It also requires something more valuable: a management willing to listen and act on what it hears, even at the price of extensive travel in a typically far-flung service organization.

COMMUNICATION

At Delta Airlines, top management meets all employees in groups of twenty-five to thirty at least every eighteen months. At United Airlines, the management continues to practice what its former president and chief executive officer, Edward E. Carlson, liked to call "visible management." As he has said, "If you're willing to get out and be a part of visible management . . . you learn how employees feel about their company. Then you can try to create a program where they believe in you."[27]

To insure that employees know what's going on, United backs up its personal communications with a daily *Employee Newsline* and a monthly employee newspaper. Of more interest is its *Supervisors' Hotline*, a biweekly newsletter that both informs supervisors and encourages them to communicate accurate information in the *Hotline* to those who report to them. If emulation is a form of high regard, this program is held in very high regard by other service firms.

Bill Marriott, Jr., still spends nearly half of his time in the field, listening and then talking to employees. The sequence is important. In addition to other forms of in-house communication such as newsletters, the company conducts annual attitude surveys of all employees. One Marriott executive calls it "our 'early warning system.'"[28] It is preceded by meetings explaining the purpose of the anonymously filled-out questionnaire. Two weeks after the survey, a meeting is held to announce actions taken as a result of the discussion. All this takes a lot of management time, but at Marriott, as in other leading firms, they think it pays off.

Marriott's program of feedback and action also includes Fair Treatment, a policy predating and exceeding the federal government's Equal Opportunity legislation of the 1960s. It begins with a written statement of what the company expects of its employees and of the obligations it has to them, and it provides for a grievance procedure whereby employees who are not satisfied with their supervisors can take complaints to an ombudsman without fear of retribution. These complaints can sometimes involve the highest levels of management.

Sam Walton, chairman and chief executive officer of Wal-Mart, still spends the majority of his working time in the field. As he has said, "The key is to get into the store and listen to what the associates have to say."[29]

Each top management (staff) committee at People Express includes an advisory council made up of selected customer service, flight, and maintenance managers from each of the company's organizational levels. Its entire governance structure is designed to foster participation and communication.

Perhaps the extreme in organized communication with employees can be found in the heavy maintenance operations of Swissair, a highly regarded international airline operator. The complexities of overhauling the airframe of a wide-bodied jet are so great that management meets *each morning* with small groups of employees to discuss both problems and ways of improving procedures. Here again, management's emphasis is on listening.

Finally, nearly all of the senior executives of these firms maintain an open-door policy, giving employees at all ranks access to their offices. They usually ask employees to make sure their supervisors are aware of the visit, but awareness of an open-door policy makes the supervisors more sensitive to effective communication.

POSITIVE REINFORCEMENT

Successful motivators seek out ways of providing positive reinforcement to subordinates. At Delta, every issue of *Delta Digest*, the company's monthly publication for employees, sets the tone for all managers by including a page of citations given employees who have proved particularly compassionate toward passengers in need of help. The process of identifying such actions is well-known to all employees.

The Marriott Corporation maintains a performance appraisal system in which an employee's performance is appraised at least annually by the next higher two levels of supervision. According to one senior executive, "We try to use [these reviews] to focus on strengths rather than weaknesses."[30] The process extends upward to the president, who reports to the board of directors on manpower planning and appraisal for two levels of management below him.

COMPENSATION

All of these companies mentioned have some of the most liberal and complete programs of fringe benefits in their respective industries. When possible, these companies pay wages that exceed union scale, and although the primary motive may not be to discourage unions on the property, it does remove one possible argument for union organizers. More important, nearly all the companies encourage broad stock ownership by employees in addition to their participation in profit-sharing programs. G. Michael Hostage, then of Marriott, said, "I have even known bellmen to strike up a conversation about Marriott stock on the way to the room; one reason for this being that a large number of our employees own company stock."[31]

The result of these comprehensive motivation programs is that employees do not inevitably turn to unions, even though the companies are among the most visible potential targets for union organizers in their industries. One former active and militant International Association of Machinists member said after his company was acquired by Delta: "Listen, if we needed a union here at Delta, we'd have a union. But the way they treat you, we don't need one."[32] Even where unions are present in these firms, they have often agreed to flexible work rules that allow an employee to rotate among jobs, a factor of great importance in achieving competitive advantage because it encourages more stable employment and higher productivity.

CULTURE

A corporate culture is the sum of many things, only a few of which can be touched on here. It certainly includes the values of a company's leaders, their willingness to state such values clearly to employees and customers, and the manner in which they practice their values.

In recent years, ServiceMaster, a company engaged in hospital housekeeping services, has provided the highest return on equity of all major service and manufacturing firms. The company's very name is associated with management's values and carries a double meaning: Master of Service, and Service to the Master. According to one account:

> Founded by a devout Baptist, the late Marion E. Wade, the company has always described itself as driven by religious principle. The first of its corporate objectives is "to honor God in all we do." Each annual report contains that message and a Biblical passage (1982: "Show me the path where I shall go, O Lord; point out the right way for me to walk," Psalms 25:4). The cafeteria wall at ServiceMaster's suburban headquarters proclaims that "Joy cometh in the morning," and though there are no "Cleanliness is next to godliness" signs around, the neatness and shine of the office project the thought. A cab driver who often takes ServiceMaster executives to and from airports says he occasionally hears a four-letter word, but that basically the crowd conforms to its principles: "There's nothing sneaky about them; everybody's honest; nobody lies."[33]

At People Express, Donald Burr:

> wanted People Express to serve as a role model for other organizations, a concept which carried with it the desire to have an external impact and to contribute to the world's debate about "how the hell to do things well, with good purpose, good intent, and good results for everybody. To me, that's good business, a good way to live. It makes sense, it's logical, it's hopeful, so why not do [it]?"[34]

These values have consistently included an honest concern for people: employees and customers above all else. They also embody an emphasis on conservation of financial strength as well as of the company's resources.

CONSERVATION

Delta Airlines has had one of the most conservative balance sheets in its industry, thus enabling it to weather poor operating years and to maintain employees on its rolls at times when competitors are furloughing theirs. The same is true at United Parcel Service, where the company's managers receive relatively modest pay, relying on company stock accumulated during their long-term employment to provide them with security in retirement. Bill Marriott, Jr., flies coach on business, thereby making it difficult for other executives in the company to deviate from the policy. ServiceMaster carries not one penny of debt. People Express's officers share uncarpeted offices. And Wal-Mart's headquarters are modest, as are those of many of the most successful firms whose names have been cited repeatedly. Examples of these similarities may be widely found.

LEGENDS

Peters and Waterman cite the importance of legends, particularly concerning senior executives who acted independently in the face of company policy on new product or business development in the most successful companies they observed.[35] Most of their observations were of manufacturing companies, yet legends are important in service firms as well. They usually concern operating achievements that illustrate some important element of a company's values and policies, and they involve either customers or employees. Legends provide the stuff out of which company lore is spun, and they communicate more graphically and memorably than any set of policies those qualities an organization seeks in its managers and employees.

Sometimes the lore results from unplanned activities. Executives at United Parcel Service tell this story:

> A few days before Christmas, a railroad official called the Chicago office of United Parcel Service of America, Inc. and confessed that a flatcar carrying two UPS trailers had unaccountably been left on a siding in the middle of Illinois. UPS is no Santa Claus, but it tries its best to deliver Christmas packages on time. So the regional manager paid for a high-speed diesel that whipped that flatcar into Chicago ahead of an Amtrak passenger train, and he ordered two of UPS's fleet of 24 Boeing 727s diverted to Chicago to get the contents of their trailers to their destinations in Florida and Louisiana in time for Christmas. In spite of the extraordinary expense, the manager neither asked permission nor even informed UPS headquarters in Greenwich, Connecticut, until weeks later.
>
> "We applauded it when we heard about it," says Kent C. Nelson, UPS vice president for customer service. "We give these guys complete authority to run their operations and do their jobs. We push decision-making down to the lowest possible levels."[36]

Sometimes such lore is orchestrated. In the fast-food business, senior managers can often be found during busy periods helping out in a unit. They have some assurance that word of their effort will get around the chain. Joe Rogers, Jr., president of Waffle House, has spent more than one New Year's Eve "filling in" on the grill of one of his firm's units. Senior executives at Shoney's, a fast-growing chain in the Southeast, regularly do the same. Managers at Delta can sometimes be found handling baggage during busy holiday periods. All the managers of Swissair's Maintenance and Engineering group recently turned out to help convert the airline's entire fleet of aircraft to a three-class service configuration, which required installing hundreds of new seats.

At Citicorp, the stories that have become part of the company's lore concern risk-taking by executives, whether they succeeded or failed. One of the most widely told these days is about the ability of John Reed, the recently named chairman, to persevere in the face of huge losses in his Individual Banking division. According to one report, the losses "earned him the wrath of both Wall Street and managers in other parts of the bank, who were angry about losing their bonuses because Reed's red ink was draining Citi's profits."[37] The eventual success of the division probably earned him his new job.

Obviously there is a pay-off from all this, but conversations with "legendary" senior managers reveal that they rarely engage in such activities out of a cynical desire to manipulate their colleagues to achieve better results. They are genuinely interested in "being where the action is" at times when they know their subordinates are under stress. They remember the experience when they were coming up through the ranks.

ESTABLISHING AND MAINTAINING THE SERVICE MENTALITY

Schlumberger and ServiceMaster are both leaders in their respective industries, outstanding performers by any measure that might be applied to them. They present contrasts as well.

The Schlumberger field engineer is highly trained and backed by the latest technology. He serves an oil well driller who places a high value on the engineer's advice concerning the likely success of the drilling venture. The ServiceMaster housekeeper is rarely well-educated and performs housekeeping tasks that the customer organization, often a hospital, does not want to manage itself.

The two companies' similarities appear in their managers' enthusiasm for running their businesses. Backgrounds may differ, but they continue to find challenges in what they are doing and convey a real sense of satisfaction in being able to deliver a necessary service successfully. These are important elements of a service mentality.

Just as managers of successful manufacturing firms must believe in what their firms make, managers of leading service firms must believe strongly in the value of what their firms do. The challenge is to communicate their conviction and enthusiasm to others in non-management positions.

Many managers of large, successful service organizations have confided, "this basically is a simple business," but they manage to maintain over time an enthusiasm not explained by high compensation or other factors. Without exception, these managers like people, and they make sure that they have fun in their jobs, often injecting variety and excitement. By so doing, they make their firms more exciting and interesting places for employees "on the firing line."

Sam Walton, president of Wal-Mart, recently danced a hula on Wall Street in full dress appropriate for the occasion. He had promised he would do the dance if his firm exceeded a high profit goal for the year. A senior executive of operations for the 800-store Brooks Fashion Store chain has become known in the company for his personally prepared videos that communicate the rules of each new sales contest to store managers and employees. Employees who await them with high expectations are rarely disappointed. A short time ago a new dress sales contest was announced by someone portraying Boy George who strangely resembled their boss. Superfluous hi-jinks? These executives and many like them use such devices to maintain their own enthusiasm and that of others in the firm. Along the way, they contribute to company legends and lore.

These managers understand that the service mentality of a firm's employees at all levels needs constant polishing, just like a long-running Broadway play. Some have concluded that the cast may need to be changed a bit more often than in other types of firms. At Marriott, employees are given an attractive retirement program that encourages many to retire with substantial income after thirty years of service, often before reaching their fiftieth birthday.

However it is achieved, success in the service industries belongs

to managers and employees who can share the excitement of working with people and who insure that even the most menial of
services are performed well, even seeing no more tangible a result
than a customer's smile. Managers and employees who enthusias-
tically deliver good service derive a great deal of satisfaction from
it and have fun.

These results are not achieved without a great deal of time and
effort. The senior vice president for finance at Delta remarked
recently that "I would guess 25% of the time of the finance department officers is spent listening to people problems."[38]

Even this level of attention may not always be enough. One
recent study involving some of Delta's flight attendants has
pointed out the great potential for alienating service workers from
their customers, their employers, and even themselves when they
are compelled to deliver personal services in ways that require
them to suppress their true feelings over long periods of time.[39]

Successful managers of human resources have known for some
time what research is just beginning to document. Recent research
suggests direct relationships between:

- The design of successful service encounters—through employee selec-
  tion, training, customer preconditioning, facility layout, efficient equip-
  ment, or other efforts—and service employee satisfaction.[40]
- Management emphasis on serving customers (instead of imposing rules
  and procedures) and service employee satisfaction.[41]
- Successful service encounters and service employee motivation.[42]
- Satisfied service employees and satisfied customers.[43]
- Satisfied customers and an increased volume of business.[44]

Managers in these firms understand that an effective human
resource program consists of doing many little things right. They
have therefore spent considerable time building programs that are
very difficult to duplicate and that in themselves represent significant barriers to entry.

CHAPTER EIGHT

The Multinational Development of Service Industries

Restaurant goers in Texas can eat at a Maxim's of Paris. In Paris they can eat at a McDonald's. Travelers in Boston can stay at a Meridien Hotel, operated by a subsidiary of Air France. Travelers in Nairobi can stay at a Hilton Hotel. These visible evidences of the multinational growth of services represent only the tip of the iceberg.

The Midland Bank, one of England's largest, has established a worldwide business based in Switzerland to specialize in brokering multiparty transactions in which firms without sufficient currency exchange can barter their goods. Browning-Ferris, based in Houston and the second largest waste management business in the United States, is expanding its overseas business by following its major competitor, Chicago-based Waste Management, Inc., into the Saudi Arabian and Kuwaiti markets. Hospital Corporation of America operates facilities in eight countries. Of the first 55,000 patients attracted to the well-publicized heart surgery unit at St. Luke's Episcopal Hospital in Houston, about 4,000 were from the Netherlands alone. And the Sheraton Corporation manages the Great Wall Hotel of Peking, under contract to China International Travel Service and its American investor-partner.

Several years ago the world's two largest advertising agencies,

Tokyo-based Dentsu, Inc. and Young & Rubicam Inc. of New York, formed a joint venture to market their multinational services not only in Japan and the United States but in many other markets of the world. Their joint venture, DYR, opened its first office in Kuala Lumpur, Malaysia. With billings of more than $100 million in 1982, the venture is expected to grow rapidly. From its California offices, DHL Corporation recently announced a major campaign to obtain a share of the overnight package delivery business in the United States. The major reason the announcement was regarded with more than casual interest by other operators in the industry was that DHL Corporation is a subsidiary of DHL Worldwide Courier Express Network, a company formed in 1969 to capture what has turned out to be the largest share of the multinational courier service market, providing reliable service between business centers and areas of the world having poor communications. Also recently, Nomura Securities Company of Tokyo sold its customers 2.2 million shares of IBM stock worth more than $270 million as part of a program to import American stocks to Japan and vice versa. The company earned more than any other investment banker in the world in 1983. Its current president, Setsuya Tabuchi, stated, "I think that perhaps half of our business will be international, not in my time, but in that of my successor."[1]

World trade in services is growing rapidly. In spite of stringent restrictions placed on some aspects of this trade, its growth has been irrepressible and of strategic importance to many major service firms.

THE NATURE OF MULTINATIONAL SERVICE TRADE

How important is the world trade in services? Information is sketchy, of limited reliability, and requires considerable interpretation. One estimate, provided by an agency of the U.S. government, claims the trade in services represented about 30 percent of total world trade in 1980, with more than a sixfold increase in value in just fifteen years.[2] Data compiled by the United Nations, graphed in Figure 8-1, suggest that it has remained near 26 percent of total trade for all non-Communist-bloc countries. The exception is the dip in 1974 caused by the rapid escalation in oil prices throughout the world.

World trade in services during the past decade has been of great

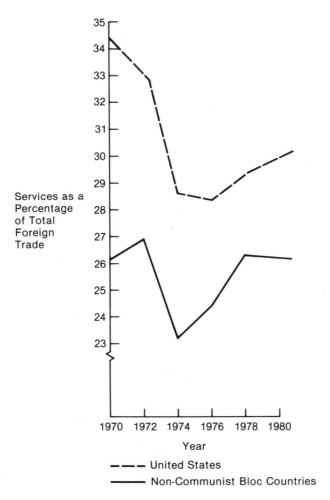

Figure 8-1
Foreign Trade in Services in the U.S. and Non-Communist-Bloc Countries,
1970–1980

importance to the United States. The favorable balance of trade in services displayed in Figure 8-2 has offset all or much of the large unfavorable balances of trade in products until 1981.

Data on world trade in services are much less accurate than those for goods. According to one claim, "There are 10,000 different classifications for reporting imports and exports in goods. Yet only six classifications exist for reporting service transactions."[3]

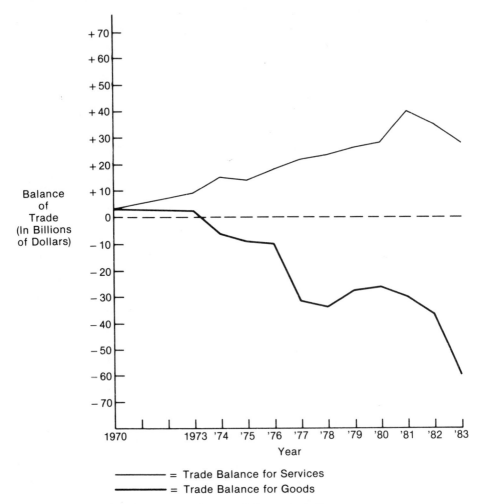

Figure 8-2
Trends in the U.S. Balance of Trade in Services and Products, 1970–1983

Source: U.S. Department of Commerce, *1985 Statistical Abstract*
(Washington, D.C.: U.S. Government Printing Office, 1985),
p. 800.

The somewhat elusive nature of data on service trades has hampered trade experts in their efforts to estimate the impact of government restrictions (or their relaxation) on trade in services and other economic effects. One analysis suggested:

A . . . reason that the service trade has tended to elude notice, economists say, involves its makeup. Some service-trade categories may appear familiar enough. But others reflect transactions that hardly spring to mind when the topic is trade. A few illustrations suggest the wide range:

- A West German tourist visits Chicago and his spending there shows up as a service export in the "travel" category of U.S. trade data.
- A New Yorker flies to London on British Airways and his ticket payment to the foreign carrier counts as a service import in the "passenger fares" category.
- A Japanese firm ships autos from Okinawa to Portland, Oregon, and pays for ship-handling services at the U.S. port; these count as service exports under "transportation."
- A U.S. company licenses its desalinization process to a Middle Eastern concern and the fee appears as a service export under "royalties and fees."[4] (Incidentally, the latter transaction could replace an export of product, thereby reducing product exports.)

The export of so-called "invisibles" by any country is a mixture of domestic services provided to touring foreigners: transport, communications, military, and other services supplied across borders; and income from investment (money export) in service and manufacturing operations conducted in other countries. Few of these transactions involve exports or imports in the traditional sense.

Calculated in these terms, the world trade in services has grown at a faster rate than that for goods, currently approximately 25 percent of total trade. Table 8-1 shows it to be highly concentrated. About 78 percent of the trade was represented by just fifteen countries in 1980, most of them in advanced stages of economic development. It has been an important source of net earnings for some (the United States, the United Kingdom, France, and Switzerland), and it has produced large negative service trade balances for others (Saudi Arabia, West Germany, Japan, and Brazil).[5]

For 1980, Table 8-1 shows that most of the total of $118.2 billion in U.S. service exports constituted investment income, essentially income derived from American ownership of assets abroad. This 1980 figure was nearly twice that for investment "imports," interest earned by foreign entities on investments in the United States, although the gap between these two figures appears to be narrowing.

No wonder that the United States and the United Kingdom have taken an intense interest in efforts to initiate discussions about relaxing international barriers to services.

Table 8-1
Service Trade Activity and Balances, Most Active Trading Countries, 1980[a]

Country	Share of Total Service Exports (%)	Share of Total Service Imports (%)	Amount of Surplus or Deficit, ($ Billions)
United States			
Investment Income	12.0	7.0	$30.4
Military Transactions	1.4	1.7	(2.2)
Travel and Transport	4.1	4.3	(1.0)
Other Services	2.1	.9	7.3
Total[b]	19.6	13.9	$34.1
United Kingdom	9.3	7.8	8.8
France	8.9	7.3	8.7
Switzerland	2.3	1.2	6.5
Italy	4.7	3.8	5.4
Austria	2.3	1.5	4.8
Spain	2.2	1.5	4.5
Belgium	5.6	5.4	1.6
Netherlands	4.7	4.7	(0.2)
Mexico	1.4	2.3	(5.5)
Canada	1.7	3.3	(9.7)
Brazil	.5	2.2	(10.1)
Japan	5.2	7.1	(11.4)
West Germany	8.5	10.5	(12.1)
Saudi Arabia	1.9	5.7	(23.0)
Total	78.8	78.2	$ 2.4

[a]The most active trading countries recorded more than $10 billion in services exports or imports in 1980; Communist-bloc countries were not reporting and are not included in the total.
[b]The U.S. figures do not add up to the total because detail and total are calculated differently.
Sources: 1981 Statistical Yearbook (New York: United Nations, 1983), 256–283. The United States breakdown is from *Statistical Abstract of the United States 1985*, U.S. Department of Commerce (Washington, D.C.: U.S. Government Printing Office, 1985), 802.

DETERMINANTS OF THE IMPORTANCE OF MULTINATIONAL ACTIVITY

Some services focus on offering mobility; others travel well in a cultural sense; still others are desired by customers engaged in multinational activities, particularly where the use of networks might be important. Some are treated more benignly than others by government regulators and are allowed to flourish with little restriction other than that imposed on domestic services.

"MOBILITY" OF THE SERVICE PRODUCT

Mobility is prized in international trade, whether for traveling from one place to another, or being able to move money rapidly from one country to another as a hedge against uncertainty or to reduce risk otherwise. The greatest period of growth in international trade has accompanied the greatest advances in the speed of international travel.

Money has long been recognized as the most mobile commodity in the world. Providing the desired mobility has been the basis for many of the most successful multinational service businesses.

CULTURAL TRANSFERABILITY

Markets may be more culturally indifferent to some services than to others. Distinctions between commercial and consumer markets for services abound. The world's business culture is relatively homogeneous in its needs for financing and other services. Most of the world's business community speaks at least one language in common, making it much easier to market and deliver commercial service products on a basis common to several countries. And in terms of the capability a loan provides a buyer anywhere in the world, it is no surprise that the financial services industry is one of the most advanced on the multinational front.

Consumer services travel less well. Those involving entertainment and communication must be adapted to language barriers. They involve a greater need to understand and reflect cultural and language differences in the design of the service as well as in its delivery. Food and lodging industries may be affected similarly. Non-meat-eating India represents a relatively poor national market for McDonald's. Even in commercial services that promote consumer goods, cultural differences may require careful study and accommodation. Advertising prepared for viewing elsewhere in the world, regardless of the language, may not be suitable for use in Japan. The most successful consumer advertising in Japan tends to convey an agreeable mood or theme, even though it may not mention price or where the product can be bought. Hard-hitting advertising suitable for other markets often misses the mark there.

THE IMPORTANCE OF FOLLOWING (OR LEADING)
THE CUSTOMER

Multinational services support trade in goods; they provide the infrastructure that facilitates trade. However, they may be somewhat dependent on trade activity in goods. In either case, firms providing such services have found it imperative to go where their customers do business or risk losing their customers.

The world's international airlines, both passenger and freight, follow the customer. Nomura Securities, a brokerage firm handling 16 percent of all the shares traded on the Tokyo Stock Exchange, has found that its investors wish to preserve broader alternatives, particularly at times when interest rates are significantly higher in one country than another or when economic trends differ greatly. Nomura must therefore develop its multinational capabilities.

Many banks have recognized this principle for years. Some were led reluctantly into multinational operations by their important customers. Others, like Citicorp, systematically developed their foreign capabilities. Under Walter Wriston's leadership, Citicorp built a worldwide electronic banking system. For some time, it has been the leading corporate lender on a multinational basis from its offices in ninety-five countries.

Trading companies—large, diversified organizations with diverse financing and trading capabilities often made possible by government authorization—have facilitated and benefited from increased trade in goods as well as in services. Although their growth throughout the world has not been well documented, trading companies have been most fully developed in Japan and Switzerland. Since 1984, they have risen in prominence in other parts of the Far East.[6]

Some service firms are leading their customers into multinational markets or otherwise attempting to influence the ways in which customers develop their markets. The London-based advertising agency, Saatchi & Saatchi Company, the fastest growing of the world's ten largest agencies, has built its reputation on its ability to create advertising to support so-called global products, those marketed in essentially the same form in many countries of the world. Its strategy reflects the view that firms can take advantage of the homogenization of cultural differences, life-styles, and product preferences caused by improved communications and travel by marketing a single product on a multinational basis, thus shaping tastes to a common product.[7] The Saatchi brothers argue that global marketing requires global advertising.

Saatchi's work for British Airways emphasizes the fact that the airline annually flies more passengers than the population of Manhattan. This ad shows a replica of Manhattan coming in for a landing at Heathrow Airport in London, deliberately drawing on other-worldy effects from the film, *Close Encounters of the Third Kind*. Its thirty-seven-word narration is available in twenty languages for use in thirty-five countries. Wherever it has been shown, it has been not only watched but understood by viewers who universally grasp its awe-inspiring message and the way it is delivered.

The ability to develop and advertise products worldwide should affect other service industries as well. Up to now, international retailing chains have found it difficult to succeed both in North America and Europe, not to mention Japan. Possible reasons include overcentralized decision-making, a misreading of foreign consumers' tastes, and a reluctance to rely on local expertise. Globalization, first of products and now of the way they are advertised, has been proven successful in certain cases. To that extent many in the industry believe that international retailing will follow, contrary to recent experience.[8]

The availability of multinational services may well be encouraging firms to undertake global marketing efforts.

In 1980 the International Trade Administration of the U.S. Department of Commerce documented the extent to which U.S. firms in selected service industries realized revenues outside the United States.[9] As might be expected, the importance of non-U.S. revenues is greatest to service industries with many U.S.-based multinational customers. The eight largest U.S. accounting firms realized 39.4 percent of their 1977 revenues outside the United States. Between 1974 and 1978, non-U.S. revenues of the top ten U.S. advertising agencies rose from 46.4 percent to 51.3 percent of their total. In 1975, the thirteen largest banks collectively derived 48 percent of their earnings from international business, with approximately 140 U.S. banks having significant overseas operations at the time of the study. The 400 largest U.S. construction contractors received about 23 percent of their contract awards, and the 450 largest engineering firms about 16 percent of their billings, outside the U.S. in 1978. Much of this business was a consequence of these firms following their customers.

THE IMPORTANCE OF A NETWORK IN THE SERVICE

Customers may use some services, such as familiar fast-food restaurants, all over the world. They insist on other services associated with mobility, such as transport or the ready availability of funds in an emergency. The greater the need for a multinational network, the greater the likelihood that a well-established service firm will realize a significant portion of its revenues from foreign activity.

Holders of VISA cards are mobile. Many travel internationally. The value of the card to them is directly related to their ability to use it anywhere in the world. VISA therefore had to establish and maintain a multinational network of establishments honoring the card to reflect the needs of its customer base. Its president, Dee W. Hock, views the card as a potential device "enabling 'exchange of value.'" In his view, "A consumer should be able to exchange any asset—cash on deposit, the cash value in life insurance policies, or a mortgage he holds—to pay for virtually anything, anywhere in the world."[10] While VISA's original orientation was to the United States, foreign transactions account for a rapidly growing portion of its business and now exceed 30 percent of the total. More recently, the company announced plans to implement a worldwide network of automatic teller machines (ATMs).

The technology of networks is changing so fast that it may transform multinational competition in services such as telecommunications, which up to now have been highly regulated. Overseas transmission of international telephone calls, computer data, and telex messages make up the fastest growing segment of the telecommunications business, with about a 50 percent faster growth rate than domestic telecommunications. Between North America and Europe alone, there are six major American competitors (AT&T, ITT, MCI-Western Union International, RCA, TRT, and Western Union) and three major European competitors (Cable & Wireless, France Cables & Radio, and Italcable). In collaboration with the various government agencies, including national Postal Telephone & Telegraph (PTT) authorities in European countries, this business has been somewhat controlled over the years. Now, with satellite carrier companies such as Intelsat, International

Satellite, and Orion, it is a matter of time before individual homeowners will be able to purchase low-cost receiving "dishes" to be mounted on their rooftops. The ability of the more traditional players and government authorities to control the industry will change a great deal, and then the nature of the network and access to it will be altered drastically.

GOVERNMENT POLICY

Governments around the world have played a significant role in restricting the growth of multinational services.[11] Many services have been considered critical to the well-being of a nation's citizens and to its own development, and governments have seen fit to guarantee the delivery of quality services at low prices. National chauvinism, sometimes clothed in words such as "national defense," has at times been involved. Too many of the world's nations operate their own airlines and impose restrictions on their competitors.

Significant trade imbalances have led certain countries with negative balances both to restrict services performed by foreign firms and to develop their own service industries, regardless of market demands and preferences. Yet the need for freer trade in services has gained less attention than that for goods. Finally, as Russell Lewis has suggested, the service sector is subjected to discrimination, not simply to neglect, in the hierarchy of economic activity:

> Remarkable is the attitude of indifference or hostility to invisibles displayed until very recently by British politicians, and even British professional economists. . . . The official British view was summed up in the rule which was only changed on the eve of the 1970 general election, that the Queen's Award for exports could not be given to the exporter of a service.[12]

For whatever reason, a wide variety of service trade barriers can be found around the world: discrimination against shippers wishing to transport foreign cargo, restraints on the international flow of information, the banning of operations by foreign insurance firms, and administrative delays that hinder licensing agreements. A recent report specifies examples of such practices:

- Australia will not let foreign banks open branches or subsidiaries.
- Sweden bars local offices of foreign companies from processing payrolls abroad.

- Argentina requires car importers to insure shipments with local insurance companies.
- Japanese airlines get cargo cleared more quickly in Tokyo than do foreign carriers.
- A U.S. company using American models for an advertisement in a West German magazine must hire the models through a German agency—even if the ad is being photographed in Manhattan.[13]

More than 1,000 such barriers were outlined in a recent report prepared by the Office of the United States Trade Representative.[14] Perhaps this helps explain why services make up so small a share of international trade.

Until recently, countries have been reluctant to discuss international service trade barriers. A recent paper prepared for the Overseas Development Council, a Washington-based research institute specializing in development issues, provided one explanation:

> This category of trade [referring to services] is vast and complex to negotiate. It has also proved throughout history to be a much more sensitive policy question than goods trade, often seeming to intrude upon cultures and societies. Service activities are at the very core of national development strategies and are intimately related to policies on technology, banking, and foreign investment.[15]

Another factor cited in the reluctance to discuss these issues is lack of information. Representatives of less-advanced countries assume that those with the most well-developed service infrastructure stand to benefit most from a lowering of trade barriers. There is, however, a great difference of opinion on this point.[16] In the absence of information, it is difficult to appraise the long-term effects of a freer service trade policy on individual countries. One effect is reasonably clear: The need to deliver many services with a high level of personal contact in situations favoring the employment of someone able to communicate with the customer does not require a country "importing" services to "export" jobs thereby. In many cases, the jobs stay with the market.

More generally, the possibility of taxing transborder data flows has been discussed, and some abortive attempts have actually been made to do so.[17] Current policies of the Customs Cooperation Council and the European Economic Community require charging for the value of the magnetic tape plus the cost of encoding such tapes transported across borders. Not only have the new taxing attempts exceeded such policies, they raise complicated questions about how to value as well as how to tax data.

In November 1982, for the first time, trade barriers on services were placed on the agenda of a general meeting of GATT, the eighty-eight-nation-member General Agreement on Tariffs and Trade. In the organization's previous thirty-five-year existence, its efforts had been confined to establishing codes for conduct in the trade of goods.

Preparing for the GATT meeting, the U.S. Trade Ambassador placed a high priority on reaching agreements on services trade, citing it as "perhaps the most important of the emerging trade issues."[18] The results produced were disappointing. Disputes over trade in agricultural products and the need to counter protectionist measures for manufactured goods received far more attention. Member nations therefore merely agreed to begin preparing more data on services individually to set the stage for a future renewal of the discussion. One report stated, "In the words of one . . . delegate [to the GATT meeting], the language on services is 'the nearest thing possible to a vacuum.' "[19]

GENERAL FACTORS CRITICAL TO MULTINATIONAL SUCCESS

Factors critical to the success of service firms anywhere are equally important in a multinational competitive setting. But certain of them take on particular importance and provide insight into the workings of more successful multinational service firms: an understanding of market needs and customer behavior, careful competitive positioning, local staffing, strong controls over quality and cost, and the capability to introduce new products.

UNDERSTANDING MARKET NEEDS AND CUSTOMER BEHAVIOR

Airlines that operate both domestic and international services take great pains to accommodate the differing needs of customers in markets where their product is offered. Alitalia provides three categories of service: national, international (i.e., to other European countries), and intercontinental. The largest number of national customers fly between Rome and Milan. They are interested in frequent, dependable service and little else for the one-hour flight. As might be expected, Alitalia has little competition on these routes. Intercontinentally, however, Alitalia finds itself competing with at least one other airline for each of the countries to which it flies. Furthermore, the long flight segments lend themselves to the delivery of more complex services, including meals and films, all of which offer additional means by which to compete for business. The competition is intense, especially on routes between Italy and North America. Customers on these routes are more interested in comfort, on-board service, and dependable, on-time arrivals than they are in frequent schedules.

In some ways, the international service to other European countries is the most difficult to design and operate. It involves relatively short flight times but it requires more services than on domestic flights, and its operations are conducted in competition with other carriers.

Naturally, Alitalia closely monitors the needs of its international and intercontinental customers. It also watches the activities of its competitors when it attempts to position its services effectively on dimensions its customers consider important. Recently, it reorganized its product planning and marketing organization along the lines of its major markets to become more responsive.

Banks operating internationally have found that queue procedures working well in a retail bank in England produce disastrous results in the Middle East, where there is no such custom. And while a loan may be a loan around the world, Muslims do not recognize the practice of paying interest, making it necessary for banks in Muslim-oriented markets to assess service charges that include but do not mention interest.

CAREFUL COMPETITIVE POSITIONING

Many multinational service firms operate at the pleasure of their "host" countries, often in competition with a company supported or owned by the country. The task of positioning thus acquires an extra dimension. It often leads management to ask, "In what manner, and how hard, can we compete?"

Regulations may proscribe some competitive behavior but, in their absence, effective multinational managers attempt to obtain clearer operating guidelines either through direct negotiation or through competitive efforts designed to probe the limits of a country's policies or hospitality.

LOCAL STAFFING

Staffing one's operations with nationals of the host country has proved desirable to leading service firms. It may indeed be essential in services involving a high degree of customer contact. It may also add to staffing costs, however, because of the frequent necessity to recruit multilingual employees.

All of McDonald's franchisees are nationals of the countries in which they operate outlets. And while the company maintains a common basic menu and format throughout the world, it has occasionally bowed to national tastes: It has added tea to its menu in Britain and beer in Belgium and West Germany.

CONTROL

Questions often arise in a multinational service operation about the degree to which local policies, procedures, performance measures, and reward systems should reflect local customs and needs as opposed to those of the company. At stake are basic matters of control over the quality and cost of the service delivered.

Leading service companies have tailored compensation programs to local operating locations, but they hold firm in managing by a common set of policies, procedures, and performance measures. Without these, it becomes impossible to deliver the standard service multinational customers expect. Even though Swissair maintains operating stations and ticket offices on four continents, all its employees receive the same training for their positions. They are all expected to carry out their work in the same manner and with the same results, no matter in how many different languages the tasks are accomplished.

The importance of a network can highlight the need for control and become a source of discipline for the multinational service firm. Because agents at various Swissair operating stations depend on each other for operating efficiency, they are more receptive to companywide policies and practices. But even where the network is less central to the nature of a firm's operation, surrogates can be devised to facilitate needed control, often involving peer pressure. The range is from the peer reviews or audits conducted in international advertising agencies to various incentives tying country managers' compensation to their ability to cooperate across national borders.

To enforce a common global standard of quality several years ago, McDonald's discontinued its agreement with its Paris franchise, who, it claimed, did not maintain established company standards for food quality and cleanliness. (After a protracted legal battle, the defeated franchisee opened a competing chain called O'Kitch.)

On occasion, a common level of quality can be achieved through the use of technology that restricts possibilities for deviation from a particular standard. Theodore Levitt tells the following story:

> D. Hilton Ryan, product manager of an American packaged-goods company in Europe, got impatient with a two-week wait to have new heels put on a pair of his shoes. So he and an associate designed a fast-service shoe repair facility. With no equipment available to meet the needs as they visualized them, they persuaded a manufacturer to produce equipment to their specifications. It was designed to apply two new heels and soles in less than two minutes.
>
> Then they persuaded the largest department store in Brussels to put their fast-service, while-you-wait, 40-square-foot shop into the store window on opening day. Lines formed for two blocks. Within four years they had 1,400 leased installations in department stores, railroad stations, and supermarkets all over Europe.
>
> What was the secret? They invented a speedy repair system not only in the design of the equipment, but also in the location of inventory relative to the location of the specialized department. There were seating arrangments for the while-you-wait customers so they could see the work being done. Of great importance, the system featured low-noise machines and automatic dust collectors to prevent polluting both the shop area and the surrounding store. And the prices charged the customers? Lower, of course.[20]

The elements of success of this speedy repair service, called Mister Minit, are apparent. It is adapted to the needs of the customer: to the lessor of space in which the outlets are located and to shoe-wearers feeling ill-served by shops offering slow service. Control is built in through technology that insures quality, even though the service is delivered by persons of limited skill in small units with minimal supervision.

Mister Minit, now located throughout Europe, had to overcome an additional cultural barrier confronting many service providers.

Given the speed with which it delivered its services, it had to tailor its prices to entice quality-conscious European customers to try the service.

INTRODUCTION OF NEW PRODUCTS

Successfully introducing a service new to a foreign market has depended not only on the extent to which it meets customer needs, but on whether the clientele for the service is multinational, on the degree to which the service transcends national customs, and on the importance of cultural emulation. New service-market combinations must therefore be tested more carefully in a multinational setting than in a domestic one.

Most multinational business services have been offered from a basic format, with relatively minor adjustments to meet local laws or the most rigid local customs. A multinational advertising agency must, of course, be able to communicate the desired message in a local language and within the local bounds of custom, law, or good taste. But the most successful multinational service introductions involve existing "products" offered to existing (business) clients in new markets. Automated global information services being developed by several banking organizations enable corporate treasury departments to obtain daily information on their cash positions in various currencies so that they can use their cash more efficiently and protect themselves against currency fluctuations. This extension of the cash management programs offered in domestic markets for several years requires a wedding of bankers' data bases with international information products being designed by financial publishers such as Reuter's and Dow Jones.[21]

Highly personal services have not been offered extensively worldwide. Hospital management corporations have led the way in these fields only since the early 1970s. Education remains highly nation-specific, along with many other personal services. Most such multinational services are somewhat standardized. ARA Services, Inc. recently began providing dietary food services at a Japanese hospital, the same service offered in the United States since 1952. But Japanese families, whose custom was to bring meals for hospitalized patients, had to be convinced that better treatment would result from having professionals plan and prepare the food.[22] ARA had to train Japanese managers at its Philadelphia headquarters. In the process they sold systems and expertise developed over several decades.

Even where the market for a service is indigenous, cultural emulation may play a large role in the success of a new product. Nowhere is this truer than in food service. McDonald's and its franchisees realize only a small portion of their European revenues from traveling Americans. Their customers are mostly Europeans wishing to experience something American. (If Maxim's had to rely on French customers at its U.S. restaurants, it could not survive.) By the same token, national airlines and their personnel are thought to reflect the culture and appearance of the countries they represent, providing for some passengers an opportunity to experience another culture for a few brief hours. Similarly, it may be prestigious to bank at an outlet of a foreign bank or to patronize the franchised outlet of a foreign clothing designer. The success of such introductions depends on the strength of the reputation of the service provider's home country in a particular field of endeavor.

CHAPTER NINE

Services in the Future

The service industries worldwide are entering an era in which some managers will be rewarded handsomely and others severely penalized. On balance, it will be a truly golden era for most, and more important, a golden era for those served. This is not news to managers who understand the dynamics of the times and are already taking advantage of them.

Events of the next decade will muffle concerns expressed about the deindustrialization of society, low rates of productivity increases in the service sector, and the supply of labor in future years to carry out the less attractive jobs associated with the traditional view of many service industries. Furthermore, they will underline not only the continued growth of the service sector but also the great impact of that growth on management practice and society in general.

Even though it would be foolhardy to make projections into the distant future for specific service industries, the picture is becoming more focused for several. Major forces are already at work that will have a profound impact on every one of the major industries worldwide. They are so compelling in their logic and sufficiently self-reinforcing, that while they may be slowed at times, they will not be reversed. These forces are deregulation of the service industries and the accelerated pace of technological innovation, particularly in communications and information processing.

It is quite possible that deregulation would not have occurred so rapidly without technological innovation or its promise, because technological innovation has introduced new forms of competition that have made obsolete old views about the "natural monopoly" associated with utility-like businesses making up so many of the service industries. It is also reasonable to believe that deregulation itself will speed the pace of technological innovation and its application in service industries.

DEREGULATION

Appropriately enough, the United States has been the hotbed for deregulation, and it is possible that deregulation was fathered by a fellow with the unassuming name of Fred Smith.[1] Of course, he came along at just the right time, years after the first calls for experiments involving various forms of deregulation were made by organizations with far-sighted leadership, such as the Transportation Association of America.

Fred Smith was and is an entrepreneur. Perhaps because his family had dominant interests in a transportation company, Dixie Greyhound, he applied his economics background to the industry and wrote an economics paper at Yale University in which he proposed an overnight delivery service for packages from all over the country to be flown to a central hub, sorted, and reflown to their destinations. Probably because the paper was hurriedly prepared in response to a pressing deadline, the economics professor gave Fred Smith what he later termed a deserved "gentlemanly C" on the paper. (One study was to show that Smith's approach required a package to be flown 2,258 miles on average, as opposed to 1,301 for Emery Air Freight, an important competitor operating in a more conventional network. The professor overlooked the small size and carrying cost of each package, even if flown, compared to the cost of an inefficient sorting process; hence the need for a central sorting point.)[2]

The concept continued to haunt Smith during his two tours of duty in Vietnam. Upon completion of military service, he commissioned a leading consultant to appraise the feasibility of his idea, thereby providing a possible vehicle for raising the considerable sums required to put such a service in place. Much of the rest is history. After a favorable reaction from the consultant, nearly $90 million of equity and debt was raised in several stages, in what was the largest single venture capital business start-up in history, to fund a company called Federal Express, Inc.

To imply that the company was an immediate success would be inaccurate. But within three difficult years after its founding in 1973, the company not only had achieved break-even, but was straining the limits placed on its air operations by the federal law that prohibited carriers of air freight from operating aircraft weighing more than 7,500 pounds without economic regulation. This limited the effective carrying capacity of each of the company's Falcon jets to 6,200 pounds. By 1976, the company was generating enough traffic to require the use of a squadron of such planes to and from major markets, including New York.

The thought of six or seven crews doing the work of what one could do with a larger plane disturbed Fred Smith sufficiently that he began to lobby for relaxation of the weight restriction. With the same persistence that he had previously displayed, he convinced enough legislators that the time for change was at hand. In 1977 they passed what became known as the "Federal Express Bill." The bill allowed Federal Express to fly larger planes in competition with previously regulated (and protected) carriers such as Flying Tigers, but it also opened economic competition for the entire air freight transportation industry. The experiment for which others had argued for years had become a reality.

The destruction of jobs and wealth, deterioration of service, and other disasters that had been predicted by opponents of the idea did not occur. The deregulation of the service industries in the late 1970s and early 1980s is well known, but it is impressive nonetheless, as Table 9-1 shows. One by one, transportation, financial brokerage, professional services, telephone, communications, banking, and entertainment industries have been deregulated in the United States in just a few short years.

A basic argument for deregulation is that if managers are given a greater opportunity to manage, they will deliver services more productively and of higher quality at lower prices to users. What are the results to date?

After studying air passenger transportation, one of the first industries to be deregulated, John Meyer and Clinton Oster concluded:

> In general, concerns that small communities would suffer drastic losses in air service under deregulation have proved largely un-

Table 9-1
Major Developments in the Deregulation of Service Industries in the U.S.

Year	Development
1968	The Supreme Court Carterfone decision permits non-AT&T equipment to be connected to the AT&T system
1969	The Federal Communications Commission gives MCI the right to hook its long-distance network into local phone systems
1970	The Federal Reserve Board frees interest rates on bank deposits over $100,000 with maturities of less than six months
1974	The Justice Department files antitrust suit against AT&T
1975	The Securities and Exchange Commission orders brokers to cease fixing commissions on stock sales
1977	Congress passes the "Federal Express" bill, deregulating the air freight industry
1977	Merrill Lynch offers the Cash Management Account, competing more closely with commercial banks
1978	Congress deregulates the passenger airline industry
1979	The Federal Communications Commission allows AT&T to sell nonregulated services, such as data processing
1980	The Federal Reserve System allows banks to pay interest on checking accounts
1980	Congress deregulates the trucking and railroad industries
1981	Sears, Roebuck becomes the first one-stop financial supermarket, offering insurance, banking, brokerage, and real estate services
1982	Congress deregulates the intercity bus industry
1984	AT&T agrees to divest its local phone companies; receives permission to compete in other computing and communications activities

Source: Adapted with permission from "Deregulating America," *Business Week,* November 28, 1983, © 1983 by McGraw-Hill, Inc.

founded. . . . As expected, the trunk and local service airlines have withdrawn from much of their small community service, but the commuter airlines have filled the void, typically with more frequent and more conveniently scheduled service—and at less subsidy cost to government as well.[3]

The effects have been different in each of the deregulated industries. The initial impact on service in the telephone communications industry has not been good, although it is too early to appraise long-term results. But there are several effects common to all. First, prices have been allowed to seek their own level. Some air passengers may pay more and some less, depending on the level of volume and competition on a given route. Commissions on certain stock transactions offered by the so-called discounters that sprang up after the "May Day" deregulation of the stock brokerage industry have been cut drastically. The interest that depositors receive from their banks has increased significantly.

Second, deregulation has led to a greater variety of services catering to different segments of the market for each service. Airline passengers can choose from low-cost, no-frills transportation offered by People Express and many other airlines created after deregulation. They can select the more conventional service of the long-established airlines or the luxury of services offered at some multiple of first-class fares by airlines dedicating equipment and staff to such efforts. In their study, Meyer and Oster point out that "the entrepreneurial airlines . . . have been pivotal in bringing about some of the most significant changes wrought under deregulation."[4]

Purchasers of stock may rely on a full-service, full-commission broker, or on one providing little more than transactions at a discount, or on some combination of the two. Depositors have the choice of a full range of checking and savings alternatives. Those in need of legal, dental, or other professional services can select from firms offering different prices for different levels of service, often communicated through advertising that was nonexistent before such industries were enjoined to relax self-imposed restrictions.

Third, deregulation has impressed on managers the need to manage services on the basis of better information, bringing prices into line with costs in all or most of their services. This, of course, has led to the unbundling of prices for certain services and the discontinuance of other services altogether by competitors in a given industry.

Most markedly, deregulation has required managers to manage, especially in industries that formerly were highly regulated. Those unable to respond to the newly imposed pressures have lost jobs. Companies have gone bankrupt—more than 300 in the trucking industry alone. But many more have been formed, including more than 10,000 small new trucking companies. And the survivors, both among individuals and companies, appear to be stronger for the experience. Also, as one manager after another has remarked, they are having more fun.

In industries from air transport to telephone communications, deregulation has fostered new competition aimed at smaller and more highly targeted segments of the market. While not all of these efforts will be successful, they will continue to provide a greater variety of services from which customers can select.

Notwithstanding, strong cries for reregulation will be heard from time to time. Because deregulation makes business success less predictable, leads to the relocation of jobs, and may be associated, rightly or wrongly, with undesirable business practices, it will at times incur the displeasure of managers, labor union leaders, and legislators alike. But technological development may direct reregulation toward activities different from those regulated in the past. For example, greater attention may be paid to the responsible use of information than to pricing practices.

TECHNOLOGICAL DEVELOPMENT

Services often involve a multitude of transactions, many of them small. They require the ability to process transactions rapidly and effectively (that is, inexpensively and accurately), and the ability to combine and analyze information and transmit results to managers, often hundreds of miles away. The increased speeds and accuracy levels of communications and information processing technologies, accompanied by geometrically declining costs, have had a profound impact on individual service providers.

Another interesting development is that the declining costs of such technologies have made them accessible to a growing range of competitors of all sizes. A small bank can now equip itself to offer nearly every service available to a customer of a larger, less personal bank. At roughly the same cost, and by combining efforts with other banks of modest size, it can provide the geographic reach of services desired by its customers who travel. It is quite likely that the trend toward deregulation would not have occurred if legislators and regulators had not concluded that technologies like these had so increased the ability of companies of all sizes to compete that much of the long-standing economic regulation was no longer necessary to protect either competitors or customers.

Technological change has encouraged some managers and government regulators, even in heavily regulated industries such as utilities, to think the unthinkable about possibilities for deregulation. In the utility industry, the idea of the importance of the "natural monopoly" as a way to serve the public's need for service quality and to achieve the lowest costs has long held sway. These natural monopolies have been built through a regulatory structure in the United States that guards firms against insolvency by allowing them to price on a cost-plus basis, including allowance for investment in new capacity. At the same time, of course, it has limited returns to investors. But what was regarded as a low-risk, low-return industry has become high-risk with commitments to investments in larger uneconomic facilities encouraged by the regulatory structure. While there may have been a need in the past for new capacity in some regions of the United States, there is now sufficient generating capacity to meet the needs of the economy for some years to come.

Technological change, in the form of impressively improved forms of energy distribution, has now entered the picture. There is a new willingness by industrial users and others to build their own power sources, based on improved technologies providing reasonably efficient, smaller facilities. The willingness is fueled in part by rapid rate increases made necessary by poor regulation-fostered management decisions. But the result is an increase in competition that may foster new thinking about regulation, at least at the power-generating stage. The chairman of a major utility, William W. Berry, of Virginia Electric & Power Company (Vepco), has stated flatly, "We ought to consider the idea of a deregulated industry."[5]

The importance of the new technologies is fully realized by the leadership of the most successful service companies. The president of American Airlines, Robert Crandall, says:

> There's a gigantic sociological revolution going on. To today's nine-year-olds, computers are like adding machines. We think electronic information distribution systems are going to be very important 5 to 10 years down the road. We have a very strong grasp of the new technologies. We could be the data bank for one of the videotex kinds of operations. We want to be the first airline in those systems.[6]

Managers of the service economy have been responding to the potential for applying new technologies to their businesses. New technological investment per service worker nearly doubled in real dollars between 1975 and 1982, and it appears to be increasing at the rate of about 8 percent per year.[7] Charles Jonscher estimates that "each $1,000 invested per service worker in the new technology is twice as productive as the same $1,000 invested per industrial worker in machine tools or conveyor belts."[8]

FUTURE TRENDS

What are these managers discovering that suggests the shape of the future in service industries? First, they are demonstrating new ways to substitute information for assets. Second, the new adage that "smaller is better" may apply just as often as the conventional wisdom that "bigger is better." There are, indeed, economies of small as well as large scale. Third, technologies are forcing managers to redefine their businesses, often in ways that obscure former boundaries among service industries.

Along with these first three discoveries comes an increased emphasis on the importance of maintaining flexibility and on keeping options open to take advantage of new technologies and ideas that are changing the structure of entire industries. And they are fostering new concepts of service centered on individually customized services at reasonable cost. Many industries will require that managers act now to insure integrity in the use of valuable information contained in their companies' data bases. The forces of deregulation and technological change will also have a remarkable impact on multinational competition in the service industries, stimulating such activities regardless of efforts by individual governments to stem their tide.

In the process of developing their companies and industries by these tenets, managers in the service sector may also show the way in new approaches to supervision, the organization of work, and other management practices.

SUBSTITUTING INFORMATION FOR ASSETS

Throughout the world, manufacturing is substituting information for assets. Nearly every program to reduce inventories has this character. Although less well-publicized, the same is occurring in service industries. The availability of new communication and data processing capabilities and the discovery of ways of using them effectively have made the substitution possible.

When the Girard Bank closed eighteen of its full-service branches and increased the number of its automatic teller machines (ATMs) to nearly 200 at supermarkets and other "stand-alone" sites, it increased its deposit-taking locations by 50 percent. The closings reportedly saved sufficient funds to totally defray the $5.4 million in costs associated with the ATM program. The Girard Bank was substituting information for assets.[9] (One bank estimated that the average cost of a teller transaction was $1.27, compared with 55 cents for an ATM transaction.)[10]

The rush by banks to get rid of unwanted bricks and mortar has become so great that one medium-sized New Jersey investment banking firm has created a national niche for itself by providing advice to and implementing the divestiture of unwanted branch offices.[11]

The New York-based merchandising group at Brooks Fashion Stores, a company operating about 800 women's ready-to-wear retail stores nationally, obtains category sales data daily from each store through the company's point-of-sale information system. It monitors a sample of stores in more detail in order to decide which items to reorder, sometimes only ten days after the first appearance of the merchandise in the stores. Under what it calls a system based on the "customer's vote," Brooks reorders popular items in large quantities before its competition, thereby increasing its chances of being supplied rapidly by the manufacturer. The system is absolutely vital to Brooks because the company operates one of the most successful national specialty chains without a warehouse. Brooks Fashion Stores is substituting information for assets.

Hertz and other leading auto rental agencies have implemented sophisticated inventory control programs based on more timely data from their thousands of rental desks. Hertz thereby positions its inventory more effectively, obtains greater utilization per vehicle, and reduces the need for some inventory. Hertz and its competitors are substituting information for assets.

SMALLER (AS WELL AS BIGGER) IS BETTER

In some industries, and at some stages in the delivery of services, competitors are finding that "smaller is better." Learning the lesson, managers continue to seek economies of scale at other readily available stages in the process.

Retail chains are increasing the productivity of their selling space, producing a trend among specialty store operators toward smaller stores. Benetton, an Italian-based retailer of knitted garments, is blanketing Europe and the United States with outlets that are perhaps one-tenth the size of competitors', but that achieve sales per square foot several times that of competitors. Benetton has also consolidated its shipping of finished product into one large warehouse in northern Italy, thereby achieving the benefits of centralized control over quality, automated materials handling, and shipment consolidation.[12] In so doing, it is achieving the economies of both small and large scale.

In the rush to reduce costs per seat-mile, many of the world's airlines acquired large, wide-bodied aircraft. These Boeing 747s and McDonnell DC-10s performed admirably, but their users found that if the seats could not be filled, the aircraft actually produced higher-than-expected costs per passenger seat-mile. Also, because business travelers, who dominate the world's air traffic, demand proper departure times and frequent flights, the load and schedule consolidation required by the effective use of wide-bodied aircraft worked against the process of increasing traffic.

Jan Carlzon, who became head of the Scandinavian Airlines System (SAS) several years ago, likes to compare airline seats to tomatoes. He says, "The most rotten thing in the world is a seat that takes off unsold."[13] In one year, he led a turnaround from a loss to the most profitable of Europe's airlines by, among other things, adjusting the airline's fleet assignments to meet the needs of customers better. As one account put it:

> Carlzon reckoned that SAS would sell even more seats if it stopped straining to fly unsuitable aircraft. Passengers wanted more nonstop flights, but the unwieldy airbuses were in the way. With fewer seats, DC-9s could make money flying directly from many Scandinavian cities to London or Paris. But the DC-9s were stopping at the airline's hub in Copenhagen just to funnel passengers onto the giant airbuses. Carlzon relegated the airbuses to charter work and established such nonstop routes as Oslo to Paris.[14]

Of course, wide-bodied jets continue to ply SAS's longer-distance, heavily traveled routes.

A similar question of facility size confronts nearly every power utility in the United States today. For years, the industry assumed that the more power-generating capacity that could be concentrated in one place, the greater the economies of scale. But in the 1970s, power engineers reached the point of diminishing returns from larger units by encountering problems of reliability. Even expected generating economies vanished. Stretched-out construction schedules on large plants were made necessary by objections of environmental groups. To make matters worse for those who had bet on "bigger is better" strategies, improved capabilities for transmitting excess energy from one market to another made it increasingly possible to buy energy at lower costs than a large new facility could generate.

Ironically, utilities in the fastest-growing sectors of the United States that did not heavily promote energy conservation were the ones whose managements were forced to commit to many of the newer, costlier, and bigger generating plants. Those that did not have the money to invest had to pursue alternative strategies. Consolidated Edison Company of New York has become one of the financially strongest utilities in the country by stressing energy conservation so emphatically that consumption in its service area has grown barely 1 percent annually for the last several years. Con Ed has not had to commit to ventures that have brought many other utilities to the brink of technical insolvency because of questionable construction projects that exceed the total equity of the entire industry's firms.

While large generating facilities that are already in place and operating continue to serve large markets economically, utilities are finding that they can meet the fluctuating demands of smaller markets more economically by other means.

Thus, in service industries as diverse as retailing, airline operations, and utilities, managements are proving that there are significant economies of small as well as large scale. It is interesting to note the extent to which this idea is related to the substitution of information for assets.

OBSCURING INDUSTRY BOUNDARIES

Technological change and the subsequent reassessment of business strategies will produce an unprecedented amount of inter-industry competition, obscuring traditional service industry boundaries. Some industries will merge: travel, transportation, and related services; financial services; communications; professional services; and trade (retailing and wholesaling). But even in these broad groupings, experimentation is already underway that will blur boundaries.

Both DHL International and Federal Express, small-package carriers, have begun emphasizing overnight document delivery. Both are either planning or have begun to offer electronic mail services, bringing them into competition with more conventional communications companies and postal authorities. Through a subsidiary, Merrill Lynch Communications, Inc.,[15] Merrill Lynch has become a supplier of data communications services. American Airlines has announced plans to expand greatly its telemarketing activities and to develop an electronic retailing service for owners of personal computers, which will put it solidly into merchandise retailing. And Sears, Roebuck, in addition to becoming the most profitable financial services company in recent years, is participating in several joint experiments with communications companies to explore the potential of videotex television communication technology for reaching customers electronically with its catalog operations.

Just trying to position the firms whose stocks comprise the Cambridge Services Index (see Table 2 and Figure 2 in Appendix A) on a services industry "map," as in Figure 9-1, suggests what is happening. Nearly all these companies were once positioned squarely at the center of one of these industries, but most have since repositioned themselves at the intersection of two or more industries. The increasing possibilities of interindustry competition created by developing technologies require that managers of all service enterprises periodically assess their business objectives and definitions.

IMPORTANCE OF MAINTAINING FLEXIBILITY

The experiences of Consolidated Edison illustrate another of the visible trends in service industries. Unable to commit to large, fixed investments, Con Ed found itself in a better position to take advantage of alternative technologies, such as improved distribution and the ready availability of power elsewhere in what has become virtually a national network.

A longstanding law requiring utilities to buy power from outside sources—such as industrial companies and others generating their own power—has been an incentive to users to build their own

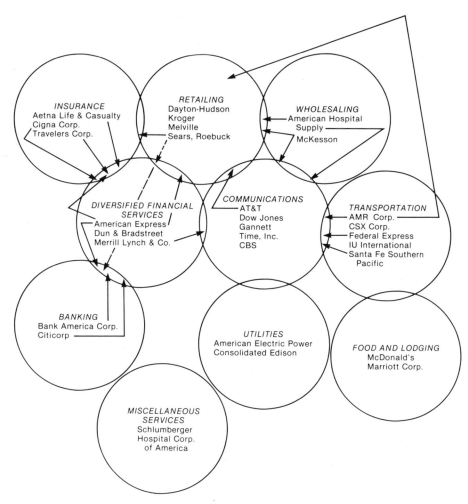

Figure 9-1
Strategic Positioning of Firms in the Cambridge Services Index

power-generating facilities. This, coupled with improved distribution technologies, has made large quantities of power available to the public through the utilities. With some foresight, and with an inadequate balance sheet at the time other utilities were committing to white elephant facilities, Con Ed's management had access to nearly twice as much power as it needed during a 1983 heat wave in the New York area.[16] It now has one of the strongest balance sheets in the industry, thanks in part to its efforts to preserve options and maintain flexibility.

In John Reed's previous position at Citicorp, before being appointed chairman, he engineered the careful development of the bank's retail banking business. A major factor in the eventual success of that business was his unwillingness to invest in traditional banking outlets. Opting instead for what appeared to some at the time to be a kind of jerry-built combination of telephones, mail, credit cards, and automated teller machines, Reed put together what he has called a "thin branch distribution network."[17] In so doing, he preserved the company's flexibility to take advantage of developing technologies and of customer attitudes toward more modern forms of banking.

THE CUSTOMIZATION OF SERVICE

Thanks to both deregulation and the development of technology, opportunities are arising for the customization of service at little additional cost. Nowhere is this more true than in services with higher information density.

By "zoning" newspapers with special advertising and copy to appeal to geographic regions of the publication's coverage, the newspaper publishing industry is evolving from one in which a publisher produces one product per day to one in which increasingly smaller segments of the population are able to receive the equivalent of customized products. Faster production and distribution processes are making this possible. Recall the "instant" book about Olympic star Carl Lewis, produced in a record-setting 41 hours and 55 minutes from manuscript to printing press after his last race in the 1984 Olympics.

A number of experiments, sponsored by well-financed pioneers such as Gannett and Time Inc., are exploring the limits of current technology as well as consumer acceptance of such customized services. These utilize technologies such as videotext, which offers an electronic newspaper from which subscribers can select whatever material is of particular interest. This form of customization, typical of many such experiments, depends on the substitution of electronics for hard copy, eliminating the need for paper. For example, Dun & Bradstreet has the capability to make its vast data base of company and personal credit information available to subscribers by electronic media.

In these efforts, heavy reliance is placed on the customer's willingness to become involved in the customization process. But nearly every such effort provides back-up services for those desiring more traditional forms of access to information.

In fact, by connecting their personal computers to various services around the world, owners can gain access to thousands of data bases, of which only a few may be of particular interest. *The Source*, owned by Reader's Digest Association, was offering its subscribers in 1984 more than 1,200 services and features, including electronic mail, computer conferencing, electronic bulletin boards, chat ("a way for fellow source members to meet and communicate electronically, often for less than the cost of a phone call"), news and sports information, and retrieval and research that provides the opportunity to order any book in print and even to obtain summaries of leading business publications.[18] Most of these services cost less than alternative methods. As if that were not enough, for a fee subscribers can also order customized research performed by more conventional methods.

DEBATE OVER THE USE OF INFORMATION

Given the importance of data as assets in many service industries, there will be increasing debate about how such information can be protected against invasions of privacy. Periodic reports of the misuse of data, including computerized data theft, may represent the greatest cloud on the horizon for many companies.

A U.S. congressional subcommittee has been considering legislation that would regulate trading in the lists that telephone marketers of all kinds use to contact potential customers. Other legislators may hold hearings on ways of limiting "junk" telephone calls associated with telemarketing, a much greater annoyance to many of their recipients than junk mail.

On the international level, there has been a growing tendency to regulate data flows. The Council of Europe Convention, preventing the infringement of individual rights to privacy through the automatic processing of name-linked data, went into effect in several European countries in 1984. The first international law on cross-border data flows, it requires that name-linked files be registered with national authorities, a process identifying "the file's name, purpose, address, where the automatic data processing is mainly carried out, and the extent to which personal data is sent abroad for automated data processing."[19] In Norway and Sweden, company visits to insure compliance have already begun.

Several companies heavily dependent on relatively free use of data have taken steps to formulate internal guidelines to insure that data are used responsibly. These guidelines usually specify that data should be used only when they benefit customers (of course, still leaving room for interpretation). For example, American Express's management has formulated a companywide Privacy Code of Conduct, containing the following statements of policy:

> We must avoid any unjustifiable intrusion on an individual's right to privacy . . . (1) obtain only that personal information which is necessary and relevant to the conduct of our business . . . (4) . . . assure that access to records is limited to those who are authorized . . . (7) advise the individual of the company's policy with respect to mailing lists and provide the individual with the opportunity to have his or her name removed from the lists. . . . The principles expressed in the Code will also govern the company's dealings with its employees.[20]

Others have insured themselves against the loss or theft of data. At least one company offering remote entry computer services, Geisco, has taken what undoubtedly will be a trend-setting step: It has engaged a large public accounting firm to monitor its standards and procedures for data security and compliance with privacy laws.

In spite of these efforts, the safest assumption is that there will be further legislation regulating the use and flow of data not in the public domain. Those most dependent on such information are already implementing carefully monitored policies for the use of data and are preparing to help shape and support legislation to reflect the needs of the public for privacy while important information services continue to be provided.

INCREASING IMPACT ON MULTINATIONAL COMPETITION

Technological change is being embraced by service industries worldwide; deregulation has not been universally received with the same enthusiasm by all governments. But the same forces making it necessary for governments and businesses around the world to adapt to technological change will make it necessary for them to adopt, or adapt to, deregulation. Neither can be contained within the boundaries of even a small number of countries, given the level of multinational service competition that already exists and the degree to which major service providers already compete under different ground rules.

Deregulation, supported by new technology, has an infectious impact on multinational competition, nowhere better illustrated than in telecommunications, financial services, and transportation.

Telecommunications. Since the development of the first message services, every country has had the equivalent of a government-owned and -operated communications service. In many countries, this authority is known as the Postal Telephone & Telegraph (PTT), supplying all forms of communication service domestically and internationally and representing a real bastion of government control.

The development of data-processing technology in a largely unregulated industry and its convergence with communications is forcing many governments to review the scope of their operations in this field. The president of GTE International, Inc., Robert J. Gressens, recently said, "They are either going to have to expand their monopoly and regulation (to include computers) or else go in the other direction and liberalize."[21]

The United States has elected to liberalize, with the deregulation of its telecommunications industry, the divestiture of various regional operating companies from their parent AT&T in 1983, and the removal of restrictions allowing these companies to enter data-processing ventures. A less publicized element of the movement is the freeing of restrictions on such firms as Western Union to allow competition for international markets.

Japan, Canada, and Great Britain are following suit. In Britain, the government recently created British Telecom, a government telecommunications service, sold it to the public, and at the same time opened the market to competition. Perhaps a good sign that the change is having its desired effects is the fact that prospective competitors are complaining that British Telecom is doing everything it can to try to maintain its monopoly. According to one account:

> British Telecom has transformed itself into a dynamic, market-oriented business that is slashing prices, offering advanced new services, and in general trying to please rather than irritate customers. For instance, waiting time for renting a new circuit in London's financial district has dropped from several months to just a few weeks.[22]

Multinational companies are locating their offices in countries such as England, that have service-oriented PTTs and relatively few restrictions on communications. This has created additional pressures for deregulation in neighboring countries.

Although many European governments, including France, staunchly maintain that the deregulation of telecommunications services would impair service or lead to increased costs for expensive-to-serve rural areas, French farmers in the south of France are participating in an experiment using videotext-oriented agricultural data services to improve their farm management techniques. And the government has chosen not to create a state monopoly in either the provision of such data bases or the manufacture of computing equipment on which they are prepared and analyzed by the farmers. Sir George Jefferson, chairman of British Telecom, suggests, "The changes in policy are driven very much by the (pace) of technology in the marketplace. In the long run, each country will make some adaptation."[23]

Financial Services. Deregulation in one financial market will inevitably lead to deregulation in another if the second wishes to remain attractive to investors. A U.S. decision to end the withholding tax on investments immediately led other countries, such as West Germany, to follow. Exchange controls have been liberalized in Britain, Japan, and Australia, adding momentum to financial deregulation in other developed countries. "Nonbank financial institutions" have sprung up in the United States and Canada in the wake of a relaxation of the interpretation of laws restricting financial services firms from engaging in banking activities. The new institutions increased foreign exchange transactions nearly sevenfold in the United States alone between 1977 and 1983. U.S. and Canadian banks are now pursuing more aggressive diversification strategies in other financial services.

More efficient markets are being demanded by users as technology is being put in place. Soon there will be 24-hour trading around the world and totally electronic trading (in addition to such traditional institutions as the securities trading floor).

According to one commentary:

> Governments and central banks in every important country are unable in some cases, unwilling in others, to resist the changes that the accelerating rate of international capital flows have thrust upon them. They do not resist the pressures to deregulate their financial systems,

because they are no longer powerful enough to do so. The quantum increase in trading of financial instruments of all kinds, and the speed at which information on which trading decisions are based is supplied to institutions and individuals everywhere, has emasculated governments' powers to regulate their domestic money and capital markets from behind barricades that were established to protect them from events elsewhere. As a result, entire financial systems, and the regulations wrapped around them, that were built in the depression era of the 1930s (in the case of the United States), and in the postwar period (as in Japan), are swept by change.[24]

Transportation. With increasing regularity, U.S. airlines are announcing new services at greatly reduced fares to points in Europe least hostile to the concept of deregulation. Unregulated companies are thus in direct competition with government-owned airlines that, along with other carriers, have long been members of the International Air Transport Association, a body that regulates international air fares. It will be interesting to see how long low-cost, unregulated competitors can remain pitted against those highly regulated by their governments, and how the situation will be resolved.

Regardless of political persuasion, the service sectors of all the world's highly developed economies are growing rapidly. More than half of all employment is now found in services. Given the vast potential demand for services worldwide and the ingenious methods for offering better, lower-cost new services, their own citizens as well as managers and representatives of other governments will increasingly demand that national governments lower barriers to competition. These demands will be more and more difficult to resist.

INFLUENCING MANAGEMENT PRACTICE

As the perceived importance of the service sector catches up with its actual importance today, managers in the service industries will be the source of most new approaches to management and the future testing ground for much of the theory concerning management practice. The railroad companies, because of their size, were the leading edge of management practice in the United States in the late nineteenth century. The best theory and practice in managing large organizations came from managers in General Motors and Du Pont when large industrial firms were ascendant in the first half of the twentieth century. Throughout this era, the engineer-manager reigned supreme, and the combination produced remarkable efforts to restructure jobs, introduce hard technologies into manufacturing, and achieve substantial gains in productivity. It was a male-dominated effort and relied on men for its labor force to a much greater degree than today. Many times it fostered a confrontational relationship between management and an increasingly organized labor force.

What of a future in which the most influential management practices may well emanate from a service sector managed by people with diverse, and often non-engineering, backgrounds? From a service sector employing a preponderant share of women? From a service sector less influenced by organized labor, a sector whose very growth in relation to industry has been responsible for a declining role for organized labor? From a service sector whose primary asset in addition to people is information rather than plant and inventory?

Gartner and Riessman have set forth some tentative hypotheses about these issues:

> It is interesting to conjecture what principles might be said to characterize a service society that would be the counterpart of industrialism's concern for quantity, incentives, bureaucratic organization, etc. Some service principles that appear to be arising might include participation, personal growth, people-oriented planning, decentralization, recurrent education, the quality of life as a central unifying goal, a positive consumerism, work autonomy, ecological constraints, demystification, consumer-intensive work.[25]

Will new organizational forms, such as those pioneered by People Express, prove to be the answer to the acute need for self-supervision, control, and personal growth in large organizations that provide high-contact personal services? Or will they instead be viewed as interesting, idealistic efforts that did not achieve their objectives? Already there are signs that People Express's management is rethinking its original vision to accommodate the strains of rapid growth.[26] Can people in the "knowledge" industries continue to be managed by principles established in an age of industrialization?[27] Or will new principles emerge?

Will the service sector be able to accommodate the natural desires of large numbers of women to develop themselves and to enter all levels of management on an equal footing with their male counterparts? Or will the strains produced by unmet expectations lead to conflict and disruption in many large firms?

Can jobs in the service sector be enhanced sufficiently to provide challenges and rewards commensurate with employees' expectations, especially in an era in which there will be pressures to contain costs, particularly labor costs, as we are now seeing in the health care industry? Or will labor in these industries turn once again to unions, this time organizing white-collar and professional rather than blue-collar membership?

Will our view of assets and ways of managing them and of accounting for them change in the service society? People and information as the cornerstones of many service industries do not lend themselves well to valuation and depreciation. Harlan Cleveland has pointed out that information, unlike most manufactured products, is often expandable (as it is used), compressible, substitutable (for capital, labor, or physical materials), highly transportable, diffusive (hard to keep secret), and sharable (as opposed to exchangeable). He concludes:

> The information resource, in short, is different in kind from other resources. So it has to be a mistake to carry over uncritically to the management of information those concepts that have proven so useful during the centuries when things were the dominant resources and the prime objects of commerce, politics, and prestige. These concepts include scarcity, bulk, limited substitutability, trouble in transporting them, and the notion of hiding and hoarding a resource.[28]

The answers to these questions probably do not lie at the extremes suggested here, but searching for them will slowly be perceived to have greater importance than searching for ways to save dying industrial firms and jobs in the world's service societies. Simon Nora and Alain Minc, perhaps in an exaggerated fashion, stated in a report to the president of France: "The liberal and Marxist approaches, contemporaries of the production-based society, are rendered questionable by its demise."[29]

CHAPTER TEN

Concluding Remarks

The so-called deindustrialization of advanced economies around the world represents an opportunity, not a threat, even to those currently employed in the industrial sector. These societies need not experience some immutable ratio between the relative levels of employment in their industrial and their service sectors. Nor is there a fixed proportion between the amounts of goods and services that organizations and people will or must consume. The greater spending power created by increased employment in service industries provides demand for the output of the industrial sector. And as manufacturers turn to others for help, producer services have been among the most rapidly growing industries. The growth of these two major sectors of economic activity is not antagonistic but complementary.

This complementary development may well change the nature of work in both sectors. There may be fewer of the high-paying jobs associated with smokestack industries that, under the very burden of high labor costs, have found it more and more difficult to compete. But there will be more jobs for more people—jobs associated with fewer environmental hazards for individuals and for society—levels of income will rise, and standards of working and leisure life will be higher.

Opinions may have differed about productivity increases in the service sector in the past, but there is increasing agreement now that the stage is set for higher growth rates in the future. A re-

spected productivity researcher, John Kendrick, concurs based on
this report:

> Services will do really well in the 1980s, Kendrick says, "and the
> stronger economic growth that results will mean a rapid rise in real
> income per capita once again. . . . "
> Greater productivity in the service sector, Kendrick predicts, will
> translate into a much slower rise in inflation in the 1980s than during
> the previous decade. . . . "A big boost in productivity is a major factor in
> the deceleration of unit labor costs," Kendrick points out. "I think this
> will mean a slowing in the prices of services themselves in the
> 1980s. . . . "[1]

In the past, higher standards of living have raised questions
about whether the pool of labor available to service providers will
shrink. Switzerland, a country with one of the highest standards of
living in the world and with one of the oldest populations, has
been importing "guest workers" for years to perform service tasks
that Swiss citizens have become increasingly uninterested in performing. But this question conceals the assumption that the nature of service jobs will remain unchanged, when in fact jobs are
rapidly being restructured. Housekeeping is a prime example of the
difficulties of changing certain service jobs, and indeed traditional
housekeeping jobs have declined faster than others in the United
States in recent years. At the same time, one of the most successful of the major service companies performs housekeeping tasks.
And the most rapidly increasing job opportunities in the service
sector are found among professional services requiring relatively
high skill levels in return for high pay.

Finally, what will increased productivity mean for employment
in the service sector? Will it dry up an important source of new
jobs? Those who harbor this fear point to the trade-off between
productivity and jobs, and make the error of extrapolating from the
specific case to the general.

Higher productivity on a job leads to more output per unit of
input. If the increased demand for output is not greater than the
increase in productivity, fewer jobs are needed. However, if the
lower prices made possible by productivity increases stimulate
demand for existing and new goods and services at a rate greater
than the productivity increase, more jobs and increased productivity can exist side by side. At the same time, of course, the very
nature of work and what constitutes productivity will change, too.

Conclusions about the future depend, then, on assumptions about the demand for services that can be delivered more productively both for other businesses (producer services) and for individuals (consumer services). There is a growing feeling that demand may be more than sufficient to create jobs, even with increasing rates of productivity. Much of the demand will be for producer services needed to maintain competitive position in a world increasingly characterized by rapid change, technological development, and domestic and multinational competition fostered by the gradual deregulation of business in the developed economies around the world.

The debate, at times ideological, concerning questions such as these, will continue. It will be fueled periodically by the emotional prospect of lost or relocated jobs in the industrial sector.[2] But it will not slow the further development of the service economy which itself is a response to the basic forces of market demand and social need.

The cornerstone of a civilized society is the willingness of people to organize themselves in ways that produce a better way of life than individuals can provide for themselves. This requires that members of the society serve each other. The Industrial Revolution opened undreamed-of possibilities for bringing people and machines together to provide a wide variety of material things at lower costs. Until recently, the technology for a service revolution was not developed sufficiently to meet exploding demands for services. More and more labor was therefore devoted to the task, and millions of jobs were created.

The service revolution has begun. It brings a vast array of more highly customized services at affordable costs, delivered with greater effectiveness and productivity. Although the proportion of jobs devoted to services may level off in the United States, the interaction between the manufacturing sector and the rapidly evolving service sectors in many other countries will continue to create jobs, albeit jobs of different content than today. Most important, service industries will help deliver the better standards of living that human beings seek. And they will offer jobs involving high levels of human interaction with significant opportunities for the self-satisfaction that comes from helping other persons.

Daniel Bell eloquently describes what this means:

If an industrial society is defined by the quantity of goods that make a standard of living, the post-industrial society is defined by the quality of life as measured by the services and amenities—health, education, recreation, and the arts—which now are deemed desirable and possible for everyone.[3]

In each of the service industries, the major players are positioning themselves to participate fully in the continued rapid growth in demand for services. It is perhaps characteristic of the dynamic quality of the service industries that some firms were founded less than twenty years ago. Others are run by senior executives with less than ten years' experience. All share an understanding of what it takes to run a highly successful service business, and they communicate that understanding to us through their actions. We could not have better teachers.

Indexes of the Growth and Importance of the Service Sector

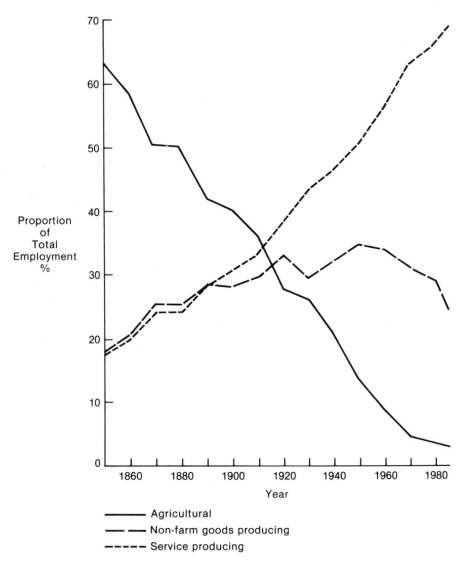

Source: U.S. Department of Commerce, Bureau of the Census *Historical Statistics of the United States* (Washington, D.C.: U.S. Government Printing Office, 1975), 137; and U.S. Department of Commerce, Bureau of the Census *Statistical Abstract of the U.S.* (Washington, D.C.: U.S. Government Printing Office, 1984), 421.

Figure A-1
Trends in U.S. Employment by Sector, 1850–1980

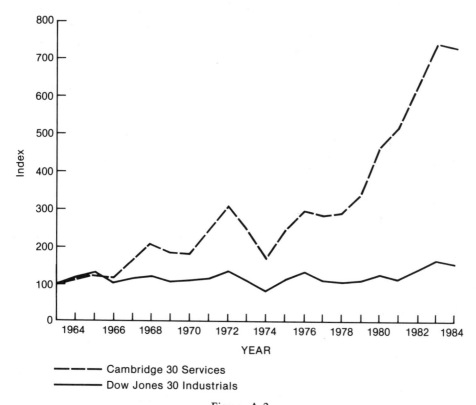

Figure A-2
Comparative Trends in the Dow Jones 30 Industrials and Cambridge 30
Services, 1963–1984

Table A-1
Rate of Growth and Relative Share of U.S. Jobs,
December 1953 to December 1983

	% of Nonfarm Jobs in December 1983	% of Nonfarm Jobs in December 1953	% Growth of Nonfarm Jobs
Service-Producing			
Finance	3.0	1.2	+383
Miscellaneous Services[a]	21.9	10.6	+282
State and Local Government	14.2	9.1	+189
Insurance	1.9	1.5	+125
Wholesale Trade	5.8	5.6	+93
Retail Trade	17.2	17.1	+86
Communications & Utilities	2.5	2.7	+73
Real Estate	1.1	1.4	+43
Federal Government	3.0	5.0	+12
Transportation	3.0	5.9	−5
Total	73.7	60.1	+127
Goods-Producing			
Construction	4.4	5.1	+62
Mining	1.1	1.6	+20
Manufacturing	20.8	33.2	+16
Total	26.3	39.9	+52
Total Jobs	92,026,000	49,693,000	+42,333,000

Source: U.S. Department of Labor, *Monthly Labor Review,* selected issues.
[a]Includes education, health, professional services, personal services, food and lodging, and others.

Table A-2
Stocks Comprising the Dow Jones Industrial and the
Cambridge Service Averages[a]

Dow Jones 30 Industrials[b]	*Cambridge 30 Services*[c]
Allied Chemical Corporation	Aetna Life and Casualty Company
Aluminum Company of America	American Electric Power Company, Inc.
American Brands, Inc.	American Express Company
American Can Company	American Hospital Supply
American Express Company	Corporation
American Telephone and Telegraph	AMR Corporation
Company	American Telephone and Telegraph
Bethlehem Steel Corporation	Company
Chevron Corporation	BankAmerica Corporation
E. I. Du Pont de Nemours &	CBS, Inc.
Company	CIGNA Corporation
Eastman Kodak Company	Citicorp
Exxon Corporation	Consolidated Edison Co. NY, Inc.
General Electric Company	CSX Corporation
General Foods Corporation	Dayton-Hudson Corporation
General Motors Corporation	Dow Jones & Co., Inc.
The Goodyear Tire & Rubber	The Dun & Bradstreet Corporation
Company	Federal Express Corporation
Inco Ltd.	Gannett Co., Inc.
International Business Machines	Hospital Corporation of America
Corporation	IU International Corporation
International Harvester Company	The Kroger Company
International Paper Company	McDonald's Corporation
Merck & Company, Inc.	McKesson Corporation
Minnesota Mining & Manufacturing	Marriott Corporation
Company	Melville Corporation
Owens-Illinois Inc.	Merrill Lynch & Company, Inc.
The Procter & Gamble Company	Santa Fe Southern Pacific Corporation
Sears, Roebuck and Co.	Schlumberger Ltd.
Texaco, Incorporated	Sears, Roebuck and Co.
Union Carbide Corporation	Time Inc.
United Technologies Corporation	The Travelers Corporation
United States Steel Corporation	
Westinghouse Electric Corporation	
F. W. Woolworth & Company	

[a]As of January 1, 1985. Both averages are calculated on the basis used for the Dow Jones 30 Industrials.
[b]Minnesota Mining & Manufacturing replaced Anaconda in 1976, IBM replaced Chrysler in 1979, Merck replaced Esmark in 1979, and American Express replaced Manville in 1982.
[c]McDonald's replaced ARA Services (Automatic Retailers) in 1966, Gannett replaced Meredith in 1968, Hospital Corporation of America replaced City Investing in 1971, Merrill Lynch replaced Transamerica in 1971, Dayton-Hudson replaced the May Company in 1976, Marriott replaced Hilton in 1976, Federal Express replaced Tiger International in 1978, CSX replaced Chessie Systems in 1980, CIGNA replaced Connecticut General in 1982, and Santa Fe Southern Pacific replaced Santa Fe in 1983.

Table A-3
Nonfarm Employment in Service Jobs, Selected Advanced
Industrial Nations, 1980

Country	Employment in Service-Producing Jobs (%)
Canada	84.0
Australia	79.3
United States	78.3
Belgium	76.0
Japan	75.1
Italy	73.4
United Kingdom	71.4
France	70.4
Federal Republic of Germany	64.6
Russia	63.7
Czechoslovakia	62.6
German Democratic Republic	52.9

Source: 1981 Statistical Yearbook (New York: United Nations, 1983), 78–82.

The Economic and Social Impact of the Service Sector

SERVICES AND RECESSIONS

During the last four recessions in the United States, employment in the service industries has increased, not fallen (see Table B-1). The total increase in service sector jobs in these recessions was not sufficient to offset declines in manufacturing employment, but without a heavy component of services the economy would have suffered more than it did. Carrying this reasoning to an extreme, one U.S. Labor Department economist remarked, "A case can be made based on job figures that an all-service economy would also be recession-free."[1]

Several reasons have been advanced for the recession-resistant nature of services. First, most services cannot be inventoried like manufactured goods. Customers for services can neither stockpile them in good times nor stop buying them during recessions. Demand for services is thereby more stable than that for manufactured goods.

This may be true for some but not for all service industries. Customers may continue to line up for banking services even though the line may shift from the deposit window to the loan desk. But retailers may experience significant softening of business, especially where purchases can be postponed. Management

Table B-1
U.S. Employment During Four Recent Recessions

Recession Period	Changes in Number of Jobs	
	Nonfarm Goods-Producing Sector	Nongovernment Service-Producing Sector
December 1969–November 1970	(1,665,000)	(10,000)
November 1973–March 1975	(2,028,000)	1,827,000
January–July 1980	(1,552,000)	277,000
July 1981–November 1982	(2,587,000)	(34,000)
Total	(7,832,000)	2,060,000

Source: U.S. Department of Labor data, as reported in the *Monthly Labor Review.*

consulting and advertising services are among the first items cut from a recession-wracked company's budget.

Second, consumers and businesses defer major expenditures during a recession, deciding instead to fix up and make do with existing appliances, machines, and the like. Thus, service jobs are substituted for manufacturing jobs.

Still another reason for recession resistance is that during hard times consumers buy more low-value, satisfaction-producing services than big-ticket manufactured products. Hair styling and shoe repair take up the slack of reduced automobile manufacture.

If these are some of the factors boosting service jobs even at the depth of a recession, why do such jobs multiply in good times as well? One important reason is that certain service can be imported only with considerable difficulty. A manufacturing firm may choose to locate a plant abroad to take advantage of lower costs for products that are then imported back into the home country for sale. But a citizen traveling abroad and buying services does not truly affect the importing or exporting of service jobs in any of the world's large developed economies. A German restaurant cannot serve an "imported" meal to a French family in France. Even if the German firm owns a restaurant in France, the service is produced primarily where it is delivered: France. And given the importance of labor in many high-contact services, much of the revenue stays with the server.

SERVICES AND PAY

With the growth of service-industry jobs in the United States many people claim that "good" (high-paying) jobs in the manufacturing sector are being replaced by lower-paying and, by implication, less challenging jobs in the service sector. Some observers who are preoccupied with the malaise of smokestack industries see the spectacular growth of the service sector as some kind of threat. Lee Iacocca, Chrysler Corporation's chairman, said recently, "We can't afford to become a nation of video arcades, drive-in banks, and McDonald's hamburger stands."[2]

This attitude suggests a lack of understanding of the significance of the service economy and of the nature of the market for its services. Not only can we afford to become a service society, we must continue our emphasis on services if firms such as Mr. Iacocca's are to flourish. A recent study for the Federal Reserve Bank of Cleveland concluded that employment for producer services—the research, engineering, data processing, and communication services that enable Chrysler and other manufacturers to remain competitive—has been increasing at a faster rate than that for the entire service sector.[3]

Nevertheless, U.S. Commerce Department data do in fact show that the average wage per full-time equivalent employee in the service sector in 1983 was $18,575. The chief economist of a New York investment banking firm notes that this wage is only about 4.6 percent below the national average for all employees. According to his analysis:

> This statistic masks a great deal of variance within the overall service sector. Workers in four of the six main areas in services—transportation and utilities, wholesale trade, finance, insurance and real estate, and government—earned more than the national average. All told, these high-wage areas accounted for half of total service employment in 1983.[4]

Moreover, low-paying service jobs in the United States have not been increasing faster than higher-paying service jobs that require more complex skills. In the most rapidly-growing segments of the U.S. service sector, hourly earnings may well be among the highest for all services. Many of these positions are dependent on interrelationships between the development of manufacturing and service segments; others reflect the relative climate for entrepreneurship so essential to the creation of new service enterprises.

The poorly based claim that lower-paying jobs are driving out "good" ones has also been used to explain why employment in Europe has not kept pace with that in the United States. According to one report:

> Many European unionists and government officials say that in any case they don't want the sorts of low paying, service-oriented jobs that are being created in the U.S. . . . Europe has created fewer jobs because productivity has increased faster than in the U.S., unions say.[5]

Regardless of the rate of pay or the relative productivity associated with the job, the fact remains that 14.7 million more people had service-sector jobs in the United States in 1984 than in 1975. But in the European Economic Community, with roughly the same size labor force, there were only about 2 million net new service-sector jobs added over the ten-year period.[6] The effect of this difference on the relative rates of unemployment for the United States and for European countries is dramatic. U.S. unemployment rates fell from 8.3 percent to 7.8 percent between 1975 and 1984, but the rate of unemployment in Europe approximately doubled.

SERVICES AND CONSUMPTION

The fact that Americans have been able to find work in the service sector has had important favorable effects on society. Most studies indicate that people with higher incomes tend to devote significantly larger proportions of their expenditures to services that contribute to what has been termed "self-identity/life-style."[7] Yet while people in developed economies appear to devote more of their resources to health and education services, consumption expenditures for other personal services have not shown similar growth.[8] Furthermore, consumers have substituted purchases of public transportation, entertainment, and housekeeping for private autos, in-home entertainment, and spare-time housecleaning. In the process, as one commentator states, "We . . . tend to take our services out in goods."[9]

SERVICES AND WORK LIFE

Services have traditionally been associated with servitude. Yet the Marriott Corporation, which operates hotels employing porters, chambermaids, and kitchen help, is ranked high by its employees in terms of quality of work life. In fact, a service firm having a high proportion of relatively menial jobs can most effectively differentiate itself from its competition through the kind of training, incentives, and recognition that lead its employees to perceive a high quality of work life. Furthermore, because of the concentration of such jobs in companies providing certain types of services, the nature of the work and the payoffs from improving it are made more visible. Entire strategies can be created with this in mind. For example, the development of systems around the universal use of lightweight plastic garbage bags has not only increased the productivity of waste disposal services; it has improved the quality of work life for their employees, thus contributing to productivity gains.

APPENDIX C

Productivity

Service jobs have been singled out as being responsible for the decreasing rate of gains in worker productivity in industrialized nations, particularly in the United States. Using such generally accepted statistics as those shown in Table C-1, some argue that service jobs with lower productivity growth have replaced manufacturing jobs with high rates of productivity growth. But questions have been raised about the applicability of productivity measures for manufacturing industries to service industries.

Productivity is determined by dividing some measure of output by a measure of input or effort. Inputs are measured in terms of labor hours worked or paid for or capital invested and generally are more easily and accurately measured than outputs. Suitable physical measures of output in all but a few service industries are more difficult to determine than in manufacturing,[1] because measures of output do not take into account variations in the quality or value of services produced. In the transportation industry, a ton-mile of output for freight delivered late receives the same weight as that for a shipment delivered on time. Labor is usually not credited for structural changes in the quality of services performed. As Michael Packer states, "Classical techniques [of productivity measurement] focus on outputs . . . rather than outcomes. . . . Traditional formulas for measuring productivity stress efficiency and neglect effectiveness."[2]

But how does one tabulate and evaluate advice provided by the

191

Table C-1
Change in Output Per Unit of Labor, by U.S. Industry Group, 1948–1979
(year-to-year % change)

	1948–79	1960–66	1966–69	1969–73	1973–79
Manufacturing	2.7	3.9	1.7	4.1	1.5
Nonfarm nonmanufacturing	1.8	2.9	1.5	1.7	0.2
Mining	1.9	5.0	4.1	0.6	(5.2)
Construction	0.6	0.8	(0.4)	(0.9)	(3.1)
Rail transport	3.3	7.3	2.0	(0.1)	1.1
Nonrail transport	1.5	2.8	2.3	3.3	1.3
Communications	5.9	5.2	4.8	4.9	5.8
Public utilities	4.9	4.8	4.8	2.7	0.6
Trade	2.5	3.9	1.1	4.3	0.8
Finance, insurance	1.0	1.0	1.7	0.4	(0.2)
Real estate	0.4	2.6	(0.2)	(1.1)	(1.4)
Other services	0.6	2.0	2.1	(1.2)	0.1
Farming	4.9	4.9	5.4	4.9	3.6
Total, private business economy	2.5	3.6	1.9	2.6	0.3

Source: John W. Kendrick, *Interindustry Differences in Productivity Growth.* © 1982 American Enterprise Institute, 12–13.

employees in a financial services firm? Economists' classical techniques cannot measure services or products for which there is no standard unit of output. Until recently there have been few efforts to publish indices for many service industries. The most extreme of the assumptions about service productivity measurement has been made in the public or government sector. Here output has been assumed to equal input, thereby creating a productivity value that by definition does not change from one period to the next. A senior economist at the Department of Commerce has remarked, "Hot dogs and productivity measures have one thing in common: you don't want to know what goes into either."

New, broader measures of productivity might allow us to make genuine comparisons between labor outputs and service outcomes. If we take into account the value, in current or deflated currency, placed on goods and services, two appropriate measures are already at hand.

The first, sales per employee, is shown for the largest manufacturing and service firms in Table 3-1. It indicates that in 1984 revenues or sales per employee in the largest service firms exceeded those of employees of the largest manufacturing firms.

An even more relevant measure is that of value added per employee, the difference between the value of sales and the value of the purchased goods and services included in each sale. Because services contain a lower percentage of purchased goods and services than manufactures, it is quite likely that the value added per employee in services is actually greater than that for manufacturing employees.

But inputs may also not be comparable. It is often assumed that productivity gains in the service sector tend to be limited because less capital is invested in it than in manufacturing. This clearly is not true for communications, transportation, and medicine. And a research office at the Federal Reserve Bank of San Francisco concluded in 1985 that the quality of data concerning capital invested in manufacturing and in service industries is not comparable. Thus, further doubt is cast on estimates attributed to trends in the productivity of either capital or labor in services.[3]

There is a continuing debate about whether the increasing proportion of total employment in the service industries is responsible for the declining rate of growth of productivity in the U.S. economy. The argument is that if nearly 80 percent of all new jobs are in service industries with lower-than-average rates of productivity growth, service jobs are responsible for creating a drag on overall productivity increases.

But the rates of growth in productivity in manufacturing businesses have declined as fast as those in services, as Table C-1 shows. Kutscher and Mark conclude from such data that the shift in employment from manufacturing to services has had a negligible effect on the decline in the growth of productivity.[4] Another prominent researcher on the subject has termed the impact "trivial."[5]

The sum of these observations conveys a different message than that drawn from more widely quoted Bureau of Labor Statistics data. Why?

First, several comparisons, such as those in Table 3-1, were based only on samples of larger firms. It's quite probable that the largest service firms have gotten where they are by being more productive. Of course, this characterizes their industrial counterparts too. Perhaps the real drag on service-sector productivity is a consequence of size. There is a relatively large number of small service firms and individual service establishments are often relatively small, even in many large service firms. Larger firms that can benefit from the introduction of productivity-improving methods will in time displace smaller firms, thereby increasing service sector productivity rates. Nevertheless, the service sector has grown in part by virtue of a large number of new business start-ups which are usually small, and services will continue to be a favorite field of opportunity for entrepreneurs.

Second, these alternative approaches measure different kinds of productivity. Output per man-hour is a measure of labor productivity in terms of quantity of goods and services produced. Value added per man-hour measures the value placed by customers on both the quality of output and its quantity. To the extent that the quality of output has improved, Bureau of Labor Statistics data probably understate productivity for both industrial and service firms.

It should be clear that existing productivity data for the service and all other sectors are subject to a great deal of interpretation.

Notes

INTRODUCTION

1. Colin Clark, *The Conditions of Economic Progress* (London: Macmillan, 1940). The tertiary sector is sometimes further divided into three parts consisting of quasi-domestic services (food and lodging), whether performed in the home or not; business services; and a "quinary" group including recreation, health care, and education, in which a central purpose is to involve and improve the customer. See, for example, Carl Gersuny and William R. Rosengren, *The Service Society* (Cambridge, Mass.: Schenkman Publishing Co., 1973). For more discussion of the problems in defining services, see Ronald Kent Shelp, *Beyond Industrialization: Ascending of the Global Service Economy* (New York: Praeger Publishers, 1981), 10–13.
2. Victor Fuchs, *The Service Economy* (New York: Columbia University Press, 1969), 16.
3. Leonard L. Berry, "Services Marketing is Different," *Business* (May-June 1980): 24.
4. Daniel Bell, *The Coming of Postindustrial Society: A Venture in Social Forecasting* (New York: Basic Books, 1973), 126–127.
5. Marvin Harris, *America Now: The Anthropology of a Changing Culture* (New York: Simon and Schuster, 1981), 179.
6. *Monthly Labor Review* (1 July 1985): 70; and *Survey of Current Business* (June 1985): 5–10.
7. *Monthly Labor Review* (1 July 1985): 70.

CHAPTER 1

1. This example is based on information in "Carrefour S.A.," HBS case no. 9–273–099 (Boston: HBS Case Services, Harvard Business School, 1973).
2. See, for example, Dennis S. Guseman, "Risk Perception and Risk Reduction in Consumer Services," in *Marketing of Services*, ed. James H. Donnelly and William R. George (Chicago: American Marketing Association, 1981), 200–204.
3. Examples of these findings include Duane L. Davis, Joseph P. Guiltman, and Wesley H. Jones, "Services Characteristics, Consumer Search, and the Classification of Retail Services," *Journal of Retailing* (Fall 1979): 3–23; and Marc G. Weinberger and Stephen W. Brown, "A Difference in Information Influences: Services versus Goods," *Journal of the Academy of Marketing Science* (Fall 1977): 389–402.
4. Christopher H. Lovelock, *Services Marketing* (Englewood Cliffs, N.J.: Prentice-Hall, 1984), 202.

195

5. Shirley Sherwood, *Venice Simplon-Orient-Express* (London: Weidenfeld & Nicholson, 1983).
6. "Wendy's Old-Fashioned Hamburgers," HBS case no. 9–677–122 (Boston: HBS Case Services, Harvard Business School, 1976).
7. For a more complete description of this firm's strategy, see "Mark Twain Bancshares," HBS case no. 9–385–178 (Boston: HBS Case Services, Harvard Business School, 1984).
8. Information for this example is drawn from "Xerox Corporation Distribution System (A)" and "Xerox Corporation Distribution System (B)," HBS case nos. 9–675–003 and 9–675–004 (Boston: HBS Case Services, Harvard Business School, 1974).
9. Jeremy Main, "Toward Service Without a Snarl," *Fortune*, 23 March 1981, 61.
10. A. Siedel, "Way Finding in Public Space: The Dallas–Fort Worth U.S.A. Airport," in *Proceedings of the Fourteenth International Conference of the Environmental Design Research Association*, ed. D. Aneseo, J. Griffin, and J. Potter (Lincoln, Nebr.: Environmental Design Research Association, 1983).
11. G. Lynn Shostack, "Planning the Service Encounter," in *The Service Encounter*, ed. John Czepiel, Michael R. Soloman, and Carol F. Surprenant (Lexington, Mass.: D. C. Heath, 1985), 252.
12. Martin R. Schlissel, "The Consumer of Household Services in the Marketplace: An Empirical Study," in *The Service Encounter*, ed. Czepiel, Soloman, and Surprenant, 303.
13. For further development of this argument, see Barry A. Blackman, "Making a Service More Tangible Can Make It More Manageable," in *The Service Encounter*, ed. Czepiel, Soloman, and Surprenant, 291–302.
14. G. Lynn Shostack, "How to Design a Service," in *Marketing of Services*, ed. Donnelly and George, 221–230.

CHAPTER 2

1. "Shouldice Hospital Limited," HBS case no. 9–683–068 (Boston: HBS Case Services, Harvard Business School, 1983).
2. For alternative conceptual schemes, see W. Earl Sasser, Jr., R. Paul Olsen, and D. Daryl Wyckoff, *Management of Service Operations* (Boston: Allyn and Bacon, 1978), 8–21; and Richard Normann, *Service Management: Strategy and Leadership in Service Businesses* (Chichester, England: John Wiley & Sons, 1984).
3. Christopher H. Lovelock, *Services Marketing* (Englewood Cliffs, N.J.: Prentice-Hall, 1984), 137.
4. "Southwest Airlines (A)," HBS case no. 9–575–060 (Boston: HBS Case Services, Harvard Business School, 1975).
5. David H. Maister, "The Psychology of Waiting Lines," in *The Service Encounter*, ed. John A. Czepiel, Michael R. Soloman, and Carol F. Surprenant (Lexington, Mass: D. C. Heath, 1985), 113–123.
6. Ken Auletta, "A Certain Poetry," Part I, *The New Yorker*, 6 June 1983, 37–55.
7. W. Earl Sasser, Jr., "Match Supply and Demand in Service Industries," *Harvard Business Review* (November-December 1976), 138.
8. Gary Knisely, "Greater Marketing Emphasis by Holiday Inn Breaks Mold," *Advertising Age*, 15 January 1979, 47–50; "Listening to Consumer is Key to Consumer or Service Marketing," *Advertising Age*, 19 February 1979, 54–60; "Financial Services Marketers Must Learn Package Goods Selling Tools," *Advertising Age*, 19 March 1979, 58–62; "Service Business Is Dealing with Other People," *Advertising Age*, 14 May 1979, 57–58.
9. "Rural/Metro Fire Department," HBS case no. 9–681–082 (Boston: HBS Case Services, Harvard Business School, 1981).

CHAPTER 3

1. For a more detailed discussion, see Michael Porter, *Competitive Strategy* (New York: The Free Press, 1980), especially 34–46.
2. David H. Maister and Christopher H. Lovelock, "Managing Facilitator Services," *Sloan Management Review* (Summer 1982): 28.
3. "Selling Financial Services From the Real Estate Office," *Business Week*, 15 October 1984, 161–162.
4. For an early discussion of decoupling, see James D. Thompson, *Organizations in Action* (New York: McGraw-Hill, 1967).
5. See, for example, Richard B. Chase, "Where Does the Customer Fit in a Service Operation?" *Harvard Business Review* (November-December 1978): 138–139.
6. Theodore Levitt, *The Marketing Imagination* (New York: The Free Press, 1983), 108–110.
7. "Ten Years of Bounding Profits," *Fortune*, 11 June 1984, 107–146.
8. Leonard L. Berry, "Services Marketing is Different," *Business* (May-June 1980): 27.
9. Ibid., 28.
10. See, for example, Christopher H. Lovelock, *Services Marketing* (Englewood Cliffs, N.J.: Prentice-Hall, 1984), 56.
11. N. W. Pope, "Mickey Mouse Marketing," *American Banker*, 25 July 1979, 4–14; and "More Mickey Mouse Marketing," *American Banker*, 12 September 1979, 4–14.
12. This is consistent with other efforts to conceptualize these relationships. See J. Richard McCallum and Wayne Harrison, "Interdependence in the Service Encounter," in *The Service Encounter*, ed. John A. Czepiel, Michael R. Soloman, and Carol F. Surprenant (Lexington, Mass.: D. C. Heath, 1985), 35–48. These authors define the terms for the equation *satisfaction = outcome–comparison level* (customer standard or expectation). They also hypothesize that unless the outcome falls below the comparison level (expectation) for an alternative service, a customer, though dissatisfied, will not switch suppliers.
13. For other examples from the lodging industry, see D. Daryl Wyckoff and W. Earl Sasser, Jr., *The U.S. Lodging Industry* (Lexington, Mass.: D. C. Heath, 1981), ix–xiv.
14. Thomas M. Block, "Innovations in Services Marketing," in *Emerging Perspectives on Services Marketing*, ed. Leonard L. Berry, G. Lynn Shostack, and Gregory D. Upah (Chicago: American Marketing Association, 1983), 23.
15. For a more complete discussion, see W. Earl Sasser, Jr., "Match Supply and Demand in Service Industries," *Harvard Business Review* (November-December 1979): 133–140.
16. For a more extensive discussion of the "membership" relationship, see Christopher H. Lovelock, "Classifying Services to Gain Strategic Marketing Insights," *Journal of Marketing* (Summer 1983): 13–14.
17. David H. Maister, "Job Assignments Set the Pace of Professional Service Firms," *Journal of Management Consulting* (Fall 1982): 32–37; and "How to Build Human Capital," *The American Lawyer* (June 1984): 6–8.
18. Theodore Levitt, "The Industrialization of Service," *Harvard Business Review* (September-October 1976): 66.
19. For a more complete description of what Benetton has done, see "Benetton (A)," HBS case no. 9–685–014 (Boston: HBS Case Services, Harvard Business School, 1984).
20. Dan R. E. Thomas, "Strategy Is Different in Service Businesses," *Harvard Business Review* (July-August 1978): 161.
21. For a more extensive discussion, see Maister and Lovelock, "Managing Facilitator Services," 21–22.
22. "Merrill Lynch's Big Dilemma," *Business Week*, 16 January 1984, 40.

23. See, for example, "Upheaval in Life Insurance," *Business Week*, 25 June 1984, 44–52.
24. "Behind the UPS Mystique: Puritanism and Productivity," *Business Week*, 6 June 1983, 66–73.
25. W. Earl Sasser, Jr., R. Paul Olsen, and D. Daryl Wyckoff, *Management of Service Operations* (Boston: Allyn and Bacon, 1978), 534–566.
26. See Eric Langeard and Pierre Eiglier, "Strategic Management of Service Development," in *Emerging Perspectives on Services Marketing*, ed. Berry et al., 68–72.
27. Richard Normann, *Service Management: Strategy and Leadership in Service Businesses* (Chichester, England: John Wiley & Sons, 1984), 97–98.

CHAPTER 4

1. Name disguised.
2. "Out of the Clouds; Back Into the Kitchen," *Forbes*, 15 May 1978, 182.
3. Carol J. Loomis, "How the Service Stars Managed to Sparkle," *Fortune*, 11 June 1984, 120.
4. Lynda Schuster, "Wal-Mart Chief's Enthusiastic Approach Infects Employees, Keeps Retailer Growing," *Wall Street Journal*, 20 April 1981, 21.
5. "The New Sears," *Business Week*, 16 November 1981, 143.
6. "How Loew's Lean Management Fattened the Profits at CNA," *Businesss Week*, 1 November 1976, 67–68.
7. "Now Airlines are Diversifying by Sticking to What They Know Best," *Business Week*, 7 May 1984, 70, 72.
8. Bill Saperito, "Kroger, the New King of Supermarketing," *Fortune*, 21 February 1983, 76.
9. "Ryder System, Inc. (B)," HBS case no. 9–573–043 (Boston: HBS Case Services, Harvard Business School, 1973).
10. "Federal Express (A)," HBS case no. 9–566–042 (Boston: HBS Case Services, Harvard Business School, 1976).
11. "Service Management: The Toughest Game In Town," *Management Practice*, Fall 1984, 8.
12. Information and quotations for this example were obtained from "The New Shape of Banking," *Business Week*, 18 June 1984, 107.
13. "Banc One Corporation and the Home Information Revolution," HBS case no. 9–682–091 (Boston: HBS Case Services, Harvard Business School, 1982), 4–5.
14. Ibid., 3.
15. "Banc One Doesn't Need Merrill Lynch," *Business Week*, 16 January 1984, 57.
16. "Banc One Corporation and the Home Information Revolution," HBS case no. 9–682–091, 13.
17. "The Iconoclast Who Made VISA No. 1," *Business Week*, 22 December 1980, 44.
18. Material in this section is adapted from James L. Heskett, "Strategies for New Product Development," *Die Unternehmung* (August 1984): 187–205.
19. Senior sponsors have variously been called "godfathers" and "executive champions." See, for example, Thomas J. Peters and Robert H. Waterman, Jr., *In Search of Excellence* (New York: Harper & Row, 1982), 208–209.
20. "The New Shape of Banking," 107–108.
21. "Marriott: The Fearless Host," *Dun's Business Month* (December 1984): 36–37.
22. Ibid.
23. Anne B. Fisher, "Dow Jones Is Still Better than Average," *Fortune*, 24 December 1984, 49.
24. Pat Wechsler Keefe, "Arthur Young's Unrewarded Virtue," *Dun's Business Month* (January 1985): 58.

CHAPTER 5

1. "The Revival of Productivity," *Business Week*, 13 February 1984, 50.
2. "A Work Revolution in U.S. Industry," *Business Week*, 16 May 1983, 103.
3. "People Express," HBS case no. 9–483–103 (Boston: HBS Case Services, Harvard Business School, 1983), 16.
4. Gary Knisely, "Greater Marketing Emphasis by Holiday Inn Breaks Mold," *Advertising Age*, 15 January 1979, 47.
5. Gary Knisely, "Service Business Is Dealing with Other People," *Advertising Age*, 14 May 1979, 57.
6. Jeremy Main, "Toward Service Without a Snare," *Fortune*, 23 March 1981, 64.
7. John Dearden, "Cost Accounting Comes to Service Industries," *Harvard Business Review* (September-October 1978): 132–140.
8. Main, "Toward Service Without a Snare," 58–66.
9. "Boosting Productivity at American Express," *Business Week*, 5 October 1981, 62, 66.
10. G. M. Hostage, "Quality Control in a Service Business," *Harvard Business Review* (July-August 1975): 102.
11. "The Medicare Squeeze Pushes Hospitals Into the Information Age," *Business Week*, 18 June 1984, 87.
12. Dearden, "Cost Accounting Comes to Service Industries," 134.
13. Howard E. McDonald and T. L. Stromberger, "Cost Control for the Professional Service Firm," *Harvard Business Review* (January-February 1969): 109–121.
14. W. Earl Sasser, Jr., "Match Supply and Demand in Service Industries," *Harvard Business Review* (November-December 1976): 133–140.
15. Theodore Levitt, "Production-Line Approach to Service," *Harvard Business Review* (September-October 1972): 44–45.
16. Ken Auletta, "A Certain Poetry," Part I, *The New Yorker*, 6 June 1983, 52.
17. Bill Saporito, "Super Valu Does Two Things Well," *Fortune*, 18 April 1983, 114–117.
18. From a speech by James Barksdale, executive vice president and chief operating officer, Federal Express, as reported in *INTECH Commentary*, March 1985, 1.
19. "The Revival of Productivity," *Business Week*, 13 February 1984, 50.
20. Christopher H. Lovelock and Robert F. Young, "Look to Consumers to Increase Productivity," *Harvard Business Review* (May-June 1979): 173.
21. Ibid., 176.

CHAPTER 6

1. Michael E. Porter, *Competitive Strategies* (New York: The Free Press, 1980), 7–33.
2. Ibid., 7.
3. William E. Fruhan, Jr., *The Fight for Competitive Advantage: A Study of the United States Domestic Trunk Air Carrier* (Boston: Division of Research, Harvard Business School, 1972).
4. See, for example, "Bucking the Trends in the World's Ailing Airline Industry," *International Management* (September 1983): 63–67; and "Singapore Airlines: Not Flying Quite So High," *Business Week*, 30 March 1981, 118.
5. Portions of this section are based on Arthur M. Louis, "VISA Stirs Up the Big Banks—Again," *Fortune*, 3 October 1983, 96, 197–199; and "Electronic Banking," *Business Week*, 18 January 1982, 70–80.
6. Louis, "VISA Stirs Up the Big Banks," 96.
7. "American Home Shield," HBS case no. 9–673–110 (Boston: HBS Case Services, Harvard Business School, 1973).
8. "How Airlines Duel With Their Computers," *Business Week*, 23 August 1982, 68–69.
9. "The New Sears," *Business Week*, 16 November 1981, 143.

10. F. Warren McFarlan, "Information Technology Changes the Way You Compete," *Harvard Business Review* (May-June 1984): 98–103.

CHAPTER 7

1. "Conrail: A Marriott Has the Inside Track," *Business Week*, 30 July 1984, 36.
2. For a discussion of this point, see W. Earl Sasser, Jr., R. Paul Olsen, and D. Daryl Wyckoff, *Management of Service Operations* (Boston: Allyn and Bacon, 1978), 400.
3. "Delta: The World's Most Profitable Airline," *Business Week*, 31 August 1981, 70.
4. Thomas Moore, "Marriott Grabs for More Room," *Fortune*, 31 October 1983, 106–122.
5. Thomas J. Peters and Robert H. Waterman, Jr., *In Search of Excellence* (New York: Harper & Row, 1982), 247.
6. Lynda Schuster, "Wal-Mart's Chief's Enthusiastic Approach Infects Employees, Keeps Retailer Growing," *Wall Street Journal*, 20 April 1982, 21.
7. "Schlumberger," *Business Week*, 16 February 1981, 66.
8. Carol J. Loomis, "How the Service Stars Managed to Sparkle," *Fortune*, 11 June 1984, 119.
9. Moore, "Marriott Grabs for More Room," 108.
10. Shawn Tully, "SAS's Festival of Profits," *Fortune*, International Edition, 30 May 1983, 73.
11. "People Express," HBS case no. 9–483–103 (Boston: HBS Case Services, Harvard Business School, 1983), 5. The information about People Express in this chapter was obtained from this source.
12. Christopher H. Lovelock et al., "Some Organizational Problems Facing Marketing in the Service Sector," in *Marketing of Services*, ed. James H. Donnelly and William R. George (Chicago: American Marketing Association, 1981), 168–171. For results of a study comparing organizational forms of British service and manufacturing firms, see also Derek F. Channon, *The Service Industries* (London: The Macmillian Press, 1978), 272–278.
13. William R. George and Hiram C. Barksdale, "Marketing Activities in the Service Industries," *Journal of Marketing* (October 1974): 65–70.
14. Lovelock et al., "Some Organizational Problems," 168–171.
15. James F. Loud, "Organizing for Customer Service," *The Bankers Magazine* (November-December 1980): 41–45.
16. P. K. Mills et al., "Flexiform: A Model for Professional Service Organizations," *Academy of Management Review* 8 (1983): 118–131; B. A. Weitz, "Effectiveness in Sales Interactions: A Contingency Framework," *Journal of Marketing* 45 (Winter 1981): 85–103; and M. Snyder, "The Self-Monitoring of Expressive Behavior," *Journal of tation," Journal Of Applied Psychology* 69, no. 1 (1984): 168.
17. Weitz, "Effectiveness in Sales Interactions," 85–103.
18. R. Dubin, I. Champoux, and L. Porter, "Central Life Interests and Organizational Commitment of Blue-Collar and Clerical Workers," *Administrative Science Quarterly* 20 (1975): 411–421.
19. G. P. Latham et al., "The Situational Interview," *Journal of Applied Psychology* 65, (1980): 322–327.
20. Joyce Hogan, Robert Hogan, and Catherine M. Busch, "How to Measure Service Orientation," *Journal Of Applied Psychology* 69, no. 1 (1984): 168.
21. Benjamin Schneider, "The Service Organization: Climate is Crucial," *Organizational Dynamics* (Autumn 1980): 52–65.
22. Ibid.
23. "Delta: The World's Most Profitable Airline," 70.
24. "Behind the UPS Mystique: Puritanism and Productivity," *Business Week*, 6 June 1983, 68.

25. G. M. Hostage, "Quality Control in a Service Business," *Harvard Business Review* (July-August 1975): 104.

26. I. Burstiner, "Current Personnel Practices in Department Stores," *Journal of Retailing* (Winter 1975): 86.

27. Edward E. Carlson, "'Visible Management' at United Airlines," *Harvard Business Review* (July-August 1975): 90–97.

28. Hostage, "Quality Control," 104.

29. Peters and Waterman, *In Search of Excellence*, 246–247.

30. Hostage, "Quality Control," 100.

31. Ibid., 103.

32. "Delta: The World's Most Profitable Airline," 71.

33. Loomis, "How the Service Stars Managed to Sparkle," 117.

34. "People Express," HBS case no. 9–483–103, 5.

35. Peters and Waterman, *In Search of Excellence*, 200–234.

36. "Behind the UPS Mystique: Puritanism and Productivity," 66.

37. "The New Shape of Banking," *Business Week*, 18 June 1984: 107.

38. "Delta: The World's Most Profitable Airline," 72.

39. Arlie Russell Hochschild, *The Managed Heart* (Berkeley: University of California Press, 1983). See also Ervin Goffman, *The Presentation of Self in Everyday Life* (Garden City, N.Y.: Doubleday Anchor Books, 1959), 208–237.

40. G. Lynn Shostack, "Planning the Service Encounter," in *The Service Encounter*, ed. John A. Czepiel, Michael R. Soloman, and Carol F. Surprenant (Lexington, Mass.: D. C. Heath, 1985), 243–253; Benjamin Schneider and David E. Bowen, "New Services Design, Development and Implementation and the Employee," in *New Services*, ed. W. R. George and C. Marshall (Chicago: American Marketing Association, 1985), 82–101.

41. See, for example, the work of J. J. Parkington and B. Schneider, "Some Correlates of Experienced Job Stress: A Boundary Role Study," *Academy of Management Journal* 22 (1979): 270–281; Warren G. Bennis, "Beyond Bureaucracy," in *American Bureaucracy*, ed. Warren G. Bennis (Chicago: Aldine, 1970), 3–17; and Peter M. Blau, *On the Nature of Organizations* (New York: John Wiley and Sons, 1974), 80–84.

42. E. E. Lawler, III, *Motivation in Work Organizations* (Monterey, Calif.: Brooks/Cole, 1973), 153–165.

43. Schneider and Bowen, "New Services Design," 82–101.

44. Eugene M. Johnson and Daniel T. Seymour, "The Impact of Cross Selling on the Service Encounter in Retail Banking," in *The Service Encounter*, ed. Czepiel, Soloman, and Surprenant, 225–239.

CHAPTER 8

1. Lee Smith, "Japan's Brokerage Giant Goes International," *Fortune*, 19 March 1984, 70–72.

2. Clyde H. Farnsworth, "GATT Talk on Barriers is Set in Geneva," *New York Times*, 23 November 1982, D1.

3. Statement by Joseph Neubauer, representing the Coalition of Service Industries, Inc., in a hearing before the Subcommittee on Trade. U.S. House of Representatives, Committee on Ways and Means, *Trade in Services and Trade in High Technology Products* (Washington, D.C.: U.S. Government Printing Office, 1982), 55.

4. Alfred L. Malabre, Jr., "Service Transactions Keep Balance of Trade in Surplus Despite the Large Deficit on Goods," *Wall Street Journal*, 10 February 1982, 54.

5. For a more complete discussion of these relationships, see Leif Edvinsson and Torgny Nandorf, "Exporting of Services: An Overview and Presentation of a Case Approach,"

in *Emerging Perspective on Services Marketing*, ed. Leonard L. Berry et al. (Chicago: American Marketing Association, 1983), 29–34.

6. See, for example, Dong Sung Cho, "Anatomy of Korean General Trading Company," *Journal of Business Research* 12, no. 2 (June 1984): 241–255.

7. See, for example, Theodore Levitt, *The Marketing Imagination* (New York: The Free Press, 1983), 20–49.

8. See, for example, David Fairlamb, "American Retreat," *Dun's Business Month* (August 1974): 69–70.

9. U.S. Department of Commerce, International Trade Administration, *Current Developments in U.S. International Service Industries* (Washington, D.C. 1980). The data in this paragraph are selected from the study. In addition, it documented data for franchising, health services, insurance, motion pictures, shipping, and tourism and air transport.

10. "The Iconoclast Who Made VISA No. 1," *Business Week*, 22 December 1980, 44.

11. For a systematic description of national and international regulation of service trade, see Ronald Kent Shelp, *Beyond Industrialization* (New York: Praeger Publishers, 1981), 99–126.

12. Russell Lewis, *The New Service Society* (London: Longman Group, 1973), 118.

13. Laura Wallace, "Global Trade Skirmish Looms as Restrictions on Services Multiply," *Wall Street Journal*, 5 October 1981, 1.

14. Ibid., 20.

15. Carlos F. Diaz-Alejandro and Gerald K. Heleiner, "Handmaiden in Distress: World Trade in the 1980's," (Washington, D.C.: Overseas Development Council, Development Paper No. 34, 1982), 2.

16. See, for example, Lewis, *The New Service Society*, and Shelp, *Beyond Industrialization*.

17. "Taxing Data Flow: It Could Be Done at Great Costs to Firms," *Business International*, 2 December 1983, 379–380.

18. Jeffrey G. Schott, "The GATT Ministerial: A Postmortem," *Challenge* (May–June 1983): 42.

19. Ibid. For other assessments, see Gilbert Simonetti, Jr., "Lowering Barriers to Trade in Services," *Best's Review* (November 1983): 28ff; and Jose Ripoll, "Should the Barriers Come Down?" *Best's Review* (November 1983): 29ff.

20. Theodore Levitt, "The Industrialization of Service," *Harvard Business Review* (September-October 1976): 71.

21. Henrietta Sender, "The Banks' New Strategy," *Dun's Business Month* (October 1984): 83–87.

22. Joseph Neubauer, "The Service Industry: Maintaining the Competitive Edge," a speech delivered to the Town Hall of Los Angeles, California, 1984.

CHAPTER 9

1. This information is based on personal conversations with Fred Smith. Opinions expressed in this section are the author's.

2. From an interview with Dr. Alan Zakon, chief executive officer of the Boston Consulting Group, reported in Paul R. Brown, "It's the Thought That Counts," *Forbes*, 21 May 1984.

3. John R. Meyer and Clinton V. Oster, Jr., *Deregulation and the New Airline Entrepreneurs* (Cambridge, Mass.: The M.I.T. Press, 1984), 199.

4. Ibid., 223.

5. "Are Utilities Obsolete?" *Business Week*, 21 May 1984, 63.

6. "American Rediscovers Itself," *Business Week*, 23 August 1982, 69.

7. "A Productivity Revolution in the Service Sector," *Business Week*, 5 September 1983, 106, 108.
8. Ibid., 106.
9. "Electronic Banking," *Business Week*, 18 January 1982, 76.
10. Orin Kramer, "Winning Strategies for Interstate Banking," *Fortune*, 19 September 1983, 118.
11. Ibid.
12. "Benetton," HBS case no. 9–685–014 (Boston: HBS Case Services, Harvard Business School, 1984).
13. Shawn Tully, "SAS's Festival of Profits," *Fortune*, 30 May 1983, 71.
14. Ibid., 73.
15. David J. Braverman, "Merrill Lynch Takes Data by the Horns," *Data Communications* (August 1983): 62–63.
16. "Are Utilities Obsolete?", 64.
17. Edward Boyer, "Citicorp After Wriston," *Fortune* 9 July 1984, 139.
18. George Shea, "The Information Explosion," *USAir* (July 1984): 54, 71.
19. "European Privacy Convention Goes Into Force in 1984," *Business Europe*, 14 November 1983, 347.
20. American Express Company, "Privacy Code of Conduct," 4 April 1978.
21. "Telecommunications: The Global Battle," *Business Week*, 24 October 1983, 127.
22. Ibid., 129.
23. Ibid.
24. Padraic Fallon, Nigel Adam, and William Allard, "The Great Deregulation Explosion," *Euromoney* (October 1984): 55. See also, for example, Peter Field, "How Deregulation Swept Australia," *Euromoney* (August 1984): 112–120; and Neil Osborn, "Canada Gets to Grips with Deregulation," *Euromoney* (November 1984): 26–36.
25. Alan Gartner and Frank Riessman, *The Service Society and the Consumer Vanguard* (New York: Harper & Row, 1974), 247.
26. John A. Byrne, "Up, Up and Away?" *Business Week*, 25 November 1985, 80–94.
27. For one of the few studies addressing these questions, see Peter K. Mills and Dennis J. Moberg, "Perspectives on the Technology of Service Operations," *Academy of Management Review* 7, no. 3 (1982): 467–478.
28. Harlan Cleveland, "Information as a Resource," *The Futurist* (December 1982): 37.
29. Ibid., 36.

CHAPTER 10

1. "A Productivity Revolution in the Service Sector," *Business Week*, 5 September 1983, 106.
2. See, for example, James Fallows, "America's Changing Economic Landscape," *The Atlantic Monthly* (March 1985): 47–68; and Peter Behr, "Shift Toward Services Continues: Observers Divided on Whether Trend Is Sapping or Bolstering U.S. Strength," *Washington Post*, 11 February 1985, F1, F3.
3. Daniel Bell, "Labor in the Post-Industrial Society," *Dissent* (Winter 1972): 1. He elaborated on this in his book, *The Coming of the Post-Industrial Society* (New York: Basic Books, 1973).

APPENDIX B

1. Alfred L. Malabre, Jr., "Service Jobs Keep Expanding in Recessions, Make Up Ever Larger Share of Work Force," *Wall Street Journal*, 15 January 1982, 44.

2. Peter Behr, "Shift Toward Services Continues," *Washington Post*, 13 January 1985, F1.
3. Robert H. Schnorbus and Lorie D. Jackson, "The Service-Sector Recovery in Cleveland," *Economic Commentary*, 10 September 1984, 3.
4. H. Erich Heinemann, "Why Not Have a Service Economy?" *Dun's Business Month* (April 1985): 68.
5. Lawrence Ingrassia, "Persistent Joblessness Still Troubles Europe in Wake of Recession," *Wall Street Journal*, 13 November 1984, 1.
6. *Yearbook of Labour Statistics, 1984* (Geneva: International Labour Organization, 1984).
7. See, for example, data presented for the United States in Thomas M. Stanback, Jr., et al., *Services, The New Economy* (Totowa, N.J.: Allanheld, Osmun & Co., 1981), 34–38.
8. *Policies for Innovation in the Service Sector* (Paris: Organization for Economic Co-Operation and Development, 1977). This study presents comparative trends in expenditures for Finland, France, Germany, Japan, Netherlands, Norway, Sweden, and the United States.
9. Thomas M. Stanback, Jr., *Understanding the Service Economy* (Baltimore: The Johns Hopkins University Press, 1979), 8. For a more complete discussion of this phenomenon in the United Kingdom, see Jonathan Gersuny, *After Industrial Society?* (London: The Macmillan Press, 1978), 71–91.

APPENDIX C

1. For descriptions of recent efforts to establish appropriate measures in various service industries, see Martin L. Marimont, "Measuring Real Output for Industries Providing Services: OBE Concepts and Methods," in *Production and Productivity in the Service Industries*, ed. Victor R. Fuchs (New York: National Bureau of Economic Research, 1969); and Frank M. Gallup and Dale W. Jorgenson, "U.S. Productivity Growth by Industry, 1947–1973," in *New Developments in Productivity Measurement*, ed. John W. Kendrick and Beatrice Vaccara (New York: National Bureau of Economic Research, 1980).
2. Michael B. Packer, "Measuring the Intangible in Productivity," *Technology Review* (February-March 1983): 53. This article provides one of the more cogent discussions of the challenges of measuring productivity.
3. Herbert Runyon, "The Services Industries: Employment, Productivity and Inflation," *Business Economics* (January 1985): 55–63.
4. Roland E. Kutscher and Jerome A. Mark, "The Service-Producing Sector: Some Common Perceptions Reviewed," *Monthly Labor Review* (April 1983): 24.
5. Edward F. Denison, *Accounting for Slower Economic Growth* (Washington, D.C.: The Brookings Institution, 1979), 46.

INDEX

Wordprocessing disks were used to edit and encode for typesetting. The book was set electronically on a Mergenthaler Linotron in Trump Medieval, designed by Georg Trump. The book was printed by offset Lithography on acid-free paper.